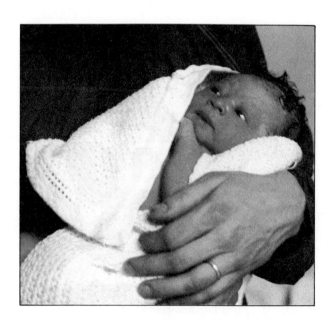

FATHER-TO-BE
Questions & Answers About
Pregnancy, Birth & the New Baby

Eric Trimmer, M.D.

TABLE OF CONTENTS

MEDICAL CONSULTANTS:
Donna Beck, M.D., Pediatrician
Anna Howard, R.N., C.N.M., Nurse Midwife
Herbert Pollock, M.D., Obstetrician-Gynecologist
Charles Rolle, M.D., Obstetrician-Gynecologist

Publisher: Rick Bailey
Editorial Director: Randy Summerlin
Editor: Judith Schuler
Art Director: Don Burton
Book Design: Leslie Sinclair
Typography: Cindy Coatsworth, Michelle Claridge
Book Manufacture: Anthony B. Narducci
Photography: Anthea Sieveking
Cover Photograph: Balfour Walker, Tucson, Arizona
Photography: Anthea Sieveking

TABLE OF CONTENTS

HPBooks®

P.O. Box 5367
Tucson, Arizona 85703
(602) 888-2150
ISBN: 0-89586-261-1
Library of Congress Catalog Card Number: 83-81100
© 1983 HPBooks, Inc.
Printed in U.S.A.
3rd Printing

©1983 Pagoda Books

The Expectant Father

Pregnancy doesn't affect *only* the woman. Both the husband and wife are expecting a baby! As a husband, you need to understand what your wife is going through so you can help her. Pregnancy will be a time of change and adjustment for you both.

Pregnancy isn't unusual—babies are born all the time. But the childbirth process often remains a mystery until we have a family ourselves. This is especially true for men.

In years past, childbearing and rearing were only for females. Today, things are changing, and fatherhood has been rediscovered. Even prior to birth, many men take an active interest in their developing offspring. Life begins before birth, and parenthood starts when the sperm meets the egg. In China, people count their age from *conception*, not the day of *birth*.

A woman values the close involvement of her husband throughout her pregnancy. You may give your wife more confidence than the top medical specialists. Parenthood isn't easy for either of you. There will be many problems to overcome.

We have collected questions fathers-to-be often ask. Answers come from many sources. They cover a wide variety of experience and opinion. You can read this book from cover to cover or read it in parts.

HPBooks has a pregnancy book for your wife, titled *Pregnant and Lovin' It*, by Lindsay R. Curtis, M.D. It covers a few of the same areas as this book, but it's written about *her*. It deals with the changes that are occurring in her body and some of the experiences she will have. The information in these books will help you both understand the changes you will experience.

The pregnancy and the birth of your child will change your marriage relationship and your attitude toward life. You may suffer certain symptoms of pregnancy—irritability, nervousness, nausea. But the rewards of fatherhood are wonderful.

You are about to start a family, or you and your wife may be having another child. The prospect of being a father can be frightening. Understanding pregnancy helps make it a healthy, happy time for you and the mother of your child.

EARLY PREGNANCY

1. *Mona's period is only 10 days overdue, but she's certain she's pregnant. How soon can we be sure?*

The first sign of pregnancy may be a missed period. But missing a period can be due to other causes, too. These include stress, anxiety, shock, anemia or hormone imbalances. If no contraception has been used during intercourse, pregnancy may be the likely cause of the missed period.

Other early symptoms of pregnancy include a feeling of fullness in the breasts, morning sickness, tiredness and a need to urinate more often than usual. Your wife may have experienced some of these symptoms.

You can't be certain until about eight days after the first day of the missed period. Your doctor will arrange a test to confirm pregnancy. By this time, the fertilized egg has begun to release a hormone, known as *human chorionic gonadotrophin*, that is passed into the urine. The hormone is detected in a urine sample taken early in the morning.

A home pregnancy-test kit can be purchased at many drugstores. Results are fairly reliable if instructions are followed closely. Your doctor will also arrange a pregnancy test.

Your wife may use a home pregnancy-test kit to detect the presence of the hormone. If the test is positive, she should see her doctor within a few weeks. He will confirm the pregnancy and give her advice about prenatal care.

2. *Diane is 14 weeks pregnant. How developed is our baby at this stage?*

Your baby can wiggle his toes and move his head, and his spine is developing. External sexual organs are already apparent.

He is about 4 inches long and weighs a few ounces. His body is covered by fine, downlike hair. From this point, growth is rapid.

3. *What is amniotic fluid, and what are its functions?*

During pregnancy, your baby is surrounded by amniotic fluid in the womb. The liquid in the amniotic cavity enables the small fetus to exercise freely as it develops. It helps the cavity and uterus to enlarge. This keeps undue pressure off the baby.

The fluid protects the fetus from injury or pressure, like a shock absorber. The fluid also provides a constant temperature for your baby. The fetus excretes substances into the fluid, including urine. Experimental studies suggest amniotic fluid is changed every few hours. The precise mechanism of this is not known.

The fetus takes in some of the fluid. This may aid development of swallowing and breathing. Some women have a lot of amniotic fluid during pregnancy, others have less. The quantity of fluid varies during pregnancy, decreasing substantially by the time the birth is due.

4. *What is an ectopic pregnancy?*

This condition is also called *tubal pregnancy.* It's a rare occurrence. The fertilized egg implants itself outside the uterus, usually in a Fallopian tube. Early symptoms include fainting, pain and bleeding. The pregnancy is not able to progress, and hospital admission is necessary. Usually the tube is removed, but repair may be possible.

If your wife has had one ectopic pregnancy, she should tell her doctor about it. He will check to see if her pregnancy is progressing normally.

5. *What is the function of the placenta?*

The placenta or *afterbirth* plays a vital part in the development of the fetus. The baby's nourishment

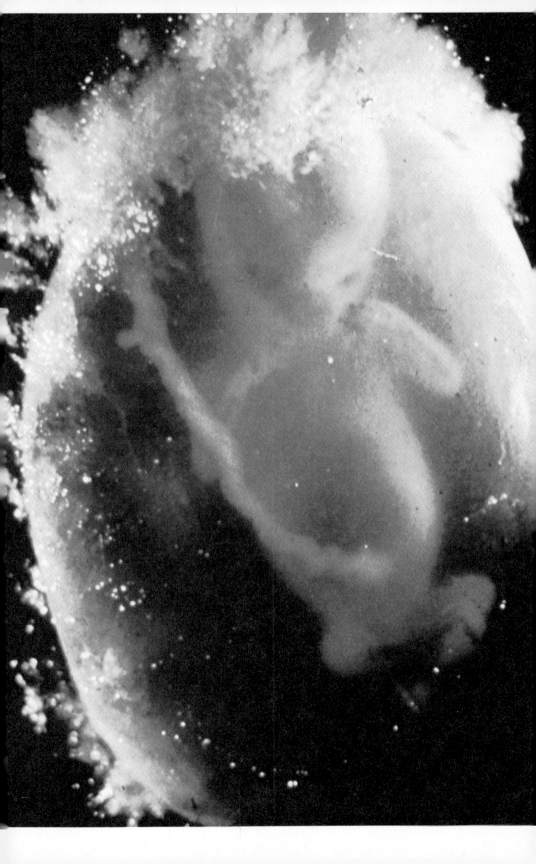

and oxygen supply pass through it. The fetal waste products also pass through it to be absorbed by the mother.

At 38 weeks, near the time of birth, the placenta measures about 7 inches across. It accounts for approximately 1/6 of your baby's weight.

You may have noticed animals eat their offspring's afterbirth. It is highly nutritious. In other parts of the world, some mothers eat the afterbirth for nutritional reasons.

6. *What is toxemia of pregnancy?*

The cause of this condition, also called *pre-eclampsic toxemia*, remains a mystery. It occurs in 5 to 10% of all pregnancies. There is no equivalent illness in any other animal.

The signs of toxemia are distinctive:
- High blood pressure.
- Excessive, rapid weight gain.
- Swelling of the hands and feet, and sometimes the face.
- Occasional kidney damage, reflected in urine tests.

Toxemia is more likely to occur in multiple births or when the pregnant woman is diabetic. Treatment for toxemia consists of dietary restrictions, bed rest and reduced salt intake. If the condition occurs, be sure your wife rests.

Regular checkups during pregnancy are important. In its worst form, pre-eclampsia becomes *eclampsia*. This can produce convulsions and even coma. Other symptoms include severe headaches, vomiting and abdominal pain. It can affect the placenta and nourishment of the unborn child if left unchecked.

Surrounded by amniotic fluid, the embryo grows into a fetus.

But this is unlikely today with advances in prenatal care. A Caesarean section or induction of labor — starting labor artificially — is important in the management of severe cases.

The presence of swollen ankles by itself does *not* indicate toxemia. This type of swelling occurs in about 70% of all pregnant women.

7. *Can we calculate when our baby will be born? I'd like to try to get time off work to help at home.*

On the average, pregnancy lasts 40 weeks, or about 280 days from the first day of the last menstrual period. Many healthy babies are born earlier or later than this. There have been advances in prenatal care in recent years, but it's still impossible to predict an exact date.

Conception can occur soon after stopping the contraceptive pill. If conception occurs in this situation, the date of birth may be incorrect. Regular menstruation may not have resumed, and you will not be able to mark the beginning of a pregnancy.

The table on the next page will help you calculate the *probable* date of birth. Look up the date of the first day of your wife's last menstrual period in column A. Column B, to the right of the date, gives the expected date of delivery. Two weeks either way allows margin for error.

BABY'S SEX

8. *We've had two boys. Now Claire and I would like a girl. Is it true my sperm determines the sex of our child?*

The sex of your child is determined at conception. The chromosome makeup of the sperm that fertilizes the egg is the important factor. So it is the man who determines the sex of his child.

How to Calculate the Birth Date

A	B	A	B
Jan1-7 .... Oct7-13		Jul2-8 .... Apr7-13	
Jan8-14 .... Oct14-20		Jul9-15 .... Apr14-20	
Jan15-21 .... Oct21-27		Jul16-22 .... Apr21-27	
Jan22-28 .... Oct28-Nov3		Jul23-29 .... Apr28-May4	
Jan29-Feb4 .... Nov4-10		Jul30-Aug5 .... May5-11	
Feb5-11 .... Nov11-17		Aug6-12 ...... May12-18	
Feb12-18 ...... Nov18-24		Aug13-19 ..... May19-25	
Feb19-25 .... Nov25-Dec1		Aug20-26 ..... May26-Jun1	
Feb26-Mar4 .... Dec2-8		Aug27-Sep2 ... Jun2-8	
Mar5-11 .... Dec9-15		Sep3-9 .... Jun9-15	
Mar12-18 ..... Dec16-22		Sep10-16 ...... Jun16-22	
Mar19-25 ..... Dec23-29		Sep17-23 ..... Jun23-29	
Mar26-Apr1 ... Dec30-Jan5		Sep24-30 ..... Jun30-Jul6	
Apr2-8 .... Jan6-12		Oct1-7 .... Jul7-13	
Apr9-15 ...... Jan13-19		Oct8-14 .... Jul14-20	
Apr16-22 ..... Jan20-26		Oct15-21 ..... Jul21-27	
Apr23-29 ..... Jan27-Feb2		Oct22-28 ..... Jul28-Aug3	
Apr30-May6 ... Feb3-9		Oct29-Nov4 ... Aug4-10	
May7-13 ...... Feb10-16		Nov5-11 ..... Aug11-17	
May14-20 ..... Feb17-23		Nov12-18 .... Aug18-24	
May21-27 ..... Feb24-Mar2		Nov19-25 ..... Aug25-31	
May28-Jun3 .... Mar3-9		Nov26-Dec2 ... Sep1-7	
Jun4-10 .... Mar10-16		Dec3-9 .... Sep8-14	
Jun11-17 ...... Mar17-23		Dec10-16 ..... Sep15-21	
Jun18-24 ...... Mar24-30		Dec17-23 ..... Sep22-28	
Jun25-Jul1 .... Mar31-Apr6		Sep24-30 ..... Sep29-Oct5	
		Dec31-Jan6 .... Oct6-12	

Use the table above to help calculate the probable date of your baby's birth. In Column A find the date of the first day of your wife's last menstrual period. Column B, to the right of the date, gives the expected date of delivery.

What you and your wife eat before the pregnancy may have some effect on the sex of your child.

9. *We are hoping our first baby will be a boy. Is it true there are steps we could have taken to ensure this?*

Statistics show about 105 boys are born for every 100 girls, so the odds are in your favor. There is no conclusive evidence to prove you can influence the sex of your child before conception. But a recent study suggested what future parents *eat* may have some effect on whether they produce a boy or a girl. Researchers claim an 88% success rate with the recommended diets.

Research into why one sex or the other is conceived is ongoing. To date, there is nothing that is considered definitive in helping plan the sex of your baby. Any steps in this direction should be taken only with your physician's agreement.

10. *Is there any way we can tell prior to the birth what the sex of our child will be?*

The results of *amniocentesis,* a test taking a sample of amniotic fluid surrounding the fetus in the womb, can reveal the sex of the baby. Some parents prefer not to be told the sex of their child in advance. A desire to know the sex of the baby prior to birth is not sufficient reason to do the test.

Some people claim there are ways of telling the sex of the unborn baby, but these are not scientific tests. They claim if you hold an object on a string above your wife's abdomen and it moves clockwise, you can count on a boy. If it moves counterclockwise, it's a girl.

The shape of the abdomen, the degree of morning sickness and the heart rate of the fetus are also thought to be indications. The presence of a certain amount of acidity in the vagina is thought by some to indicate a girl.

Some believe if intercourse occurs two or three days before ovulation, there is an 80% chance the child will be female. If intercourse occurs within a few hours of ovulation, there is an 80% chance the child will be male. One mother was convinced she was giving birth to a boy. When told she had a baby girl, she told the doctor he must be mistaken and asked him to look again!

11. *I don't understand why Susan is so anxious to have a baby girl.*

There could be many reasons why your wife wants a daughter. She may feel a child of her own sex will support her self-image as a woman. She may want a child of her own sex to have the experiences she wanted but never had. She may think a boy would be more difficult to manage.

Some women may not want a daughter if they had a difficult relationship with their own mother. They fear repeating such a pattern.

Talk with your wife about having a baby of either sex. Reassure her you will be delighted with whatever you have. She may think *you* want a daughter.

12. *Will Nancy feel different if she is carrying a boy than if she is carrying a girl?*

Some women experience more morning sickness and feel less well if they carry a girl. Some mothers of boys go through their pregnancy with no trouble at all. But there is no scientific evidence to prove this either way.

VISITING THE DOCTOR

13. *What will Sandy's first prenatal exam be like? Will she need a vaginal examination?*

The doctor will want to find out about her general state of health. He will listen to her heart and take her blood pressure.

During the internal examination, the doctor will examine the *cervix,* which is the neck of the womb. He may also take a cervical smear, or *Pap test,* a routine yearly procedure to detect abnormalities early. Your wife is probably used to this test.

The doctor will feel the softened lower part of the uterus, as well as the firmer cervix. This internal examination does not harm your baby. The doctor will be able to get an idea of the size and shape of your wife's pelvis. He will also check to see if the womb size approximates the delivery dates.

14. *At Joan's first prenatal visit, the doctor asked for details of our family medical history. Why?*

This is normal procedure. Some illnesses, such as diabetes and heart disease, can affect the pregnancy. It's important to know whether these have occurred in your family because conditions may be hereditary.

The doctor will also take details about previous pregnancies, allergies and operations.

Your wife should keep all prenatal appointments. Usually there is one appointment a month for the first six or seven months. After that, appointments will be every two weeks, and finally every week.

15. *Why do they check Ruth's blood pressure?*

Blood pressure is checked at every visit to the doctor, along with weight and urine. This is done to monitor her progress and health. A degree of fluctuation is normal in pregnancy. A significant, persistent rise may indicate *toxemia*. See page 9. Rest and treatment will be prescribed.

16. *The doctor ordered a blood test for Cindy. What will it show?*

There are several important factors that can be shown by blood tests. Your wife's blood group needs to be known, in case a transfusion is required. The test also shows whether the Rh factor, a factor found in red-blood corpuscles, is present or not. Her blood is tested for its hemoglobin content, to indicate whether your wife is anemic.

The Wasserman test indicates if syphilis is present. This test is vital because venereal disease can damage an unborn child.

Some doctors test the mother's blood for rubella or German-measles antibodies. If they are present, German-measles contact during pregnancy is not a concern. This test should be done before pregnancy. Then the woman can be vaccinated against rubella if antibodies are not present.

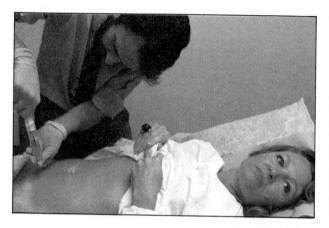

Usually a pregnant woman over 35 years of age is advised to have amniocentesis to check for signs of abnormality in the fetus. A sample of the fluid surrounding the baby is taken for analysis at 16 to 18 weeks.

17. *We are having our third child. Marsha is 39. She's going to have amniocentesis to see if the baby is developing normally. What is involved? Could there be any danger to her or the baby?*

Statistics reveal that women after age 40 are more likely to give birth to a Down's Syndrome baby. A child with Down's Syndrome is mentally retarded. Amniocentesis can reveal if this abnormality is present in the developing fetus. It may show *spina bifida,* an abnormality of the spine, and indicate whether the baby's lungs are sufficiently developed.

The amniocentesis test is a simple one. It involves slight risk to the unborn child and mother. This element of risk will be explained to you.

A local anesthetic is given, then a small sample of amniotic fluid is taken from the uterus through the abdomen. This is done around the 16th week of pregnancy.

The test is painless, and your wife can go home afterward. Results aren't available for two to three weeks. If they show an abnormality, you and your wife must decide whether to continue the pregnancy.

Don't be overly concerned about problems. Statistics of abnormality in a mother over 40 are low.

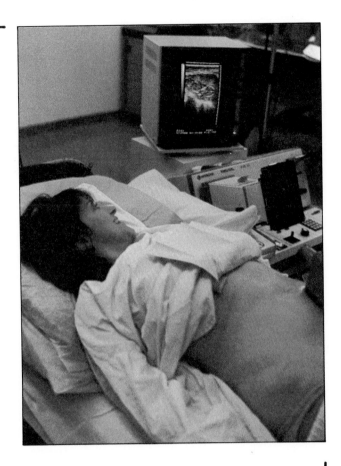

An ultrasound exam provides the first photographic portrait of your child, although the screen shows a pretty hazy image. There is little risk to your developing baby.

18. *We've been told Dina will be having an ultrasound exam next week. Is this routine? What is involved, and what will it show?*

This is also called a *sonogram* and is a safe examination. A scanner is passed over the pregnant woman's abdomen. The baby's image can be seen on a screen. Its size and position are monitored, along with the placenta. Sometimes it is done to show whether there are twins.

The technique works by use of sound waves too high to be heard. Lying flat on a table, your wife will have some oil rubbed on her stomach. This is the only part of her body that is exposed. Then the scanner is passed over her. She may be able to see on another screen the hazy outline of your child in the womb. This will be the first sight of your baby. It's an exciting experience, although the picture will look like a collection of dots, lines and dashes.

KEEPING FIT

19. *What do we need to know about medicine Dotty takes during pregnancy?*

Make it a strict rule: *Take no medicine or drug during pregnancy without consulting the doctor.* Discourage your wife from taking pills on her own. She should consult her doctor about any symptoms.

People who are addicted to some drugs give birth to babies who are also addicted. Many medicines that are not harmful to your wife can pass to the baby. Your wife should tell her doctors as soon as she suspects she is pregnant. If a doctor has prescribed something that is unsuitable, he will know.

20. *Jane keeps complaining that she can't sleep. How safe is it for her to take a tranquilizer? Is insomnia common during pregnancy?*

Your wife should *not* take any drugs during pregnancy without medical advice. Encourage Jane to see her doctor about sleep problems.

In pregnancy, sleep troubles are sometimes due to an enlarged uterus. This can cause discomfort when lying down and difficulty turning over. We all move a lot in our sleep. Your wife may be waking up

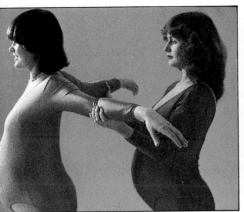

Prenatal exercises introduce your wife to certain breathing techniques. They help her develop muscle control.

because of the discomfort she feels when she changes position.

Taking a nap during the day may help her feel refreshed. Encourage her to breathe deeply when lying in bed. This helps release tension gradually from the forehead down the body. It should help bring on sleep. Getting to sleep may be helped by using relaxation exercises learned at prenatal classes.

There are some sedatives available by prescription for use in late pregnancy. Your wife's doctor will prescribe these if they are necessary.

21. *I've heard a lot about the dangers of smoking during pregnancy. Isn't it exaggerated? Will it matter if Linda smokes 10 cigarettes a day?*

Now is the time for Linda to give up smoking—her doctor will probably recommend it. She will need your support and encouragement to do it. Try putting it to her this way. Every time she lights a cigarette, the placenta's blood vessels constrict. Blood flow decreases. Your developing baby no longer receives the nourishment and oxygen needed. Consequently, birth weight may be lower than normal. Surveys show the baby of a smoking mother is about 8 ounces lighter than average at birth. The mother who smokes 20 cigarettes a day also risks having a stillborn baby.

Nicotine is a drug. No pregnant woman should use any drug without medical advice because it might damage the unborn child.

22. *Annette and I usually like to relax over a few drinks in the evening. Now that she's pregnant, will alcohol harm our baby?*

Any alcohol taken in pregnancy reaches the baby. Doctors know excessive alcohol intake can result in slow growth of a baby. It can even damage the developing brain. An occasional drink may not do any harm, but heavy drinking is out. Consult your doctor for his advice.

23. *I have heard Kathy should give up coffee during pregnancy. Is this true?*

If she enjoys a cup of coffee at breakfast or after dinner, there is probably no reason for her to give it up. If her doctor advises against coffee, she should give it up. You may find she doesn't want any coffee.

With all the new studies that are being done, your wife should check with her doctor about how different things affect the baby. Recently, there has been concern about coffee affecting a developing baby.

If she is a heavy coffee drinker, she should cut down to two or three cups a day. Research in this area is limited. However, evidence shows women who drink a lot of strong coffee may have more miscarriages than those who drink less. Caffeine may lessen the oxygen supply to the developing baby.

24. *How safe is it for Alison to ride her bicycle during pregnancy?*

It depends on how competent your wife is on her bike. If she has been riding for many years, she probably won't have any trouble. Her increasing weight and shifting center of gravity won't cause her problems. If cycling is new to her, it may be best to discourage it.

Cycling is an efficient way to get around, but think of the possibility of accidents. Her reflexes may slow a bit, so coping with traffic may become more difficult.

Swimming is good exercise during pregnancy. It's safer in a pool than in the ocean. A pregnant woman should not swim alone. She should stay out of the water if she suffers from cramps.

25. *Elizabeth has always played tennis. How safe is it for her to continue during pregnancy?*

If your wife feels fit and is used to tennis, she can continue to play. But she shouldn't get exhausted. If a woman hasn't played tennis for a long time, she should not start during pregnancy.

If your wife has put on 20 pounds, she's carrying around extra body weight equivalent to a heavy, medium-size suitcase. She needs to rest at regular intervals.

Sports like skiing, diving and horseback riding should probably be avoided. There may be too much risk of potential accidents.

Swimming is an excellent form of exercise for a pregnant woman. It involves gentle exercise of the muscles, and being in water is relaxing. But if she's in the ocean, swim with her. Don't let her go far out— she could develop a cramp.

Your wife will also get exercise when practicing the techniques she learns at prenatal classes. She will know when she should stop playing any favorite sports.

26. *Should Pauline be eating for two?*

In some ways, the pregnant woman is eating for

Good nutrition is necessary during pregnancy. The pregnant woman should eat a well-balanced diet of meat, fish, fruit, vegetables, dairy products and grains. She should avoid too much starch and processed foods. Begin to pay attention to nutrition a few months before trying to conceive.

two. She must support, with good nutrition, both her health and that of the developing baby. But it doesn't mean she needs to eat *twice* as much as normal!

Your wife should eat a well-balanced diet. It should include fiber, milk products, fresh meat and fish, fruit and vegetables. As her pregnancy continues, a woman uses less energy as she becomes less active.

Help your wife avoid rich foods. They may result in weight gain. Any unnecessary pounds may be difficult to shed afterward.

27. Should Jan be drinking a lot of milk during pregnancy? She dislikes it.

She probably doesn't need more than one pint a day, unless her diet is inadequate. Milk is popular with doctors for pregnant women because it provides many essential nutrients in one basic food. It is convenient to use milk as a food source, but it's not essential. Too much milk is fattening.

If your wife dislikes milk, she can have milk products like cheese and yogurt instead. She can also eat a large part of her daily milk in some cooked form, such as soup, pudding or sauces.

28. Why does Sandra get heartburn?

Pressure on the stomach, as well as the action of hormones during pregnancy, sometimes causes the digestive system to be sluggish. This causes heartburn. If heartburn persists, consult your doctor. He may recommend a mild antacid to help relieve discomfort. Taking regular, small meals instead of fewer large ones can also help relieve heartburn.

29. Why is it important to avoid anemia during pregnancy?

Anemia is a condition where red-blood cells become reduced in number or their hemoglobin content is reduced. Symptoms are a sore tongue, tiredness, breathlessness, pale skin tone, irritability and bad temper.

Iron is needed to form hemoglobin. The unborn child relies entirely on the iron in his mother's body to manufacture his own red-blood cells. A healthy, well-nourished, non-anemic mother supplies him with all he needs. If her iron supply is not adequate, the baby won't have enough until he gets the iron he needs from solid food. The baby may become anemic. Iron supplements are important for pregnant women.

Folic-acid anemia occurs in many woman. This substance is given as a supplement to pregnant women. It aids the development of the fetus.

30. *How important are the vitamin and iron supplements the doctor prescribed for Pat during her pregnancy?*

A woman will get most of her needed vitamins and minerals if she eats a well-balanced diet. This includes fresh meat, fish, fresh vegetables and fruit, milk and roughage from high-fiber foods.

The body needs iron during the later months of pregnancy, when the need almost doubles. The developing baby takes all nourishment from the mother's system.

It is vital for the woman to be healthy, which is why iron pills are often prescribed. Your doctor may also suggest other supplements if he feels they are necessary.

31. *How much weight should Laura gain during pregnancy?*

Opinions vary, but the average recommended gain is about 25 pounds. The average weight of a newborn baby is 7 pounds. Not all the weight gain is the baby's weight. The increase is due to additional fat deposits, weight of the enlarged breasts, amniotic fluid and the placenta.

During the first three months, there should be little weight gain. A small loss may be experienced if your wife has morning sickness. During the next 12 weeks, your wife will probably put on 7 to 12 pounds. During the last 12 weeks, she will gain about a pound a week.

Your doctor will advise her about weight gain.

Now is not the time for strict dieting. But your wife should avoid foods that are high in calories. She should eat a nutritious, well-balanced diet, high in fiber.

32. *Carol has put on a lot of weight during pregnancy. Does this mean we'll have a big baby?*

If your wife has always been large, you may have a large baby. Today's average weight for a newborn is 6 to 8 pounds. Your wife's examinations should provide an indication of your baby's size.

Sometimes a woman's apparent size during pregnancy is increased by the presence of a lot of amniotic fluid. Diabetic women tend to have large babies. Doctors want them to control their weight carefully throughout pregnancy.

Your doctor will tell your wife if he thinks she is putting on too much weight. He will give her a sensible diet.

AN EMOTIONAL TIME

33. *Sandy seems to have changed since she became pregnant. She used to be calm. Now her mood shifts. I never know what to expect next.*

This is a familiar syndrome. Almost all women experience these extremes of mood at times during pregnancy. They're on top of the world, then down in the dumps. Small, unimportant matters get out of proportion. There may be sudden bouts of weeping over nothing.

No one knows what causes these moods. They seem to be a normal aspect of pregnancy. Changes in hormonal levels are probably to blame. They may be exaggerated by certain subconscious fears.

Doing things that are relaxing and enjoyable will help your wife through her periods of irritability.

Your wife needs all the support and reassurance you can give her. Don't be surprised if she is vague, unable to concentrate or forgetful at times. These are normal during pregnancy.

You can help her through these periods of irritability. Be affectionate, and remind her it's not only the baby who matters. You love *her*. Talk about the pregnancy as a three-person thing. Help your wife prepare herself emotionally for the new role of mother. This will enhance even a close relationship.

34. *Samantha is only 17. I'm worried about how she will be able to cope with being pregnant.*

She should get adequate prenatal care as early as possible. There is no reason to assume she will encounter any particular problems. However, teen-age girls who delay seeking prenatal care have a higher risk of complications.

35. *I feel a little jealous of our unborn child. Is it normal for a man to feel this way?*

You may not be jealous of your child, but jealous of your wife's ability to bear that child. Legend has it that the god Zeus swallowed his pregnant wife to give birth to their child himself. Some psychologists suggest men subconsciously envy the experience of childbirth.

There are many subconscious anxieties that may affect the father-to-be. Will his wife reject him in favor of the baby? Will their social life disappear completely? Will he be a good father?

Financial worries may arise. Preparing for birth *together* will bring you closer. It may help you overcome doubts and fears. Your role in pregnancy is not just a background one. This is your child as much as your wife's. Close involvement in the development of your baby will help you both in this new experience.

The ability to talk about jealousy with your partner is the path to resolution. You must both be willing and able to communicate honestly. Each must be willing to listen to the other's fears and concerns and trust the other's feelings.

36. *How important is the husband's emotional support to a pregnant woman?*

The happier a woman's relationship with her husband, the easier the pregnancy will be. Mothers who are under a lot of stress during pregnancy seem to have babies with lower birth weights or babies who are irritable. Those who do not like to be

Communication with your wife will help you resolve problems you may have during the pregnancy.

pregnant are more likely to produce irritable babies. Paternal absence has an effect on the baby, too. What affects the mother may affect the baby.

Your wife needs your support during pregnancy. Help her maintain a positive outlook. You will probably both enjoy the pregnancy more. The stronger your relationship, the better the environment for your developing baby.

37. *We are concerned about our baby being normal. Are such anxieties usual?*

All parents-to-be worry during pregnancy about whether their baby will be physically and mentally normal. With today's excellent prenatal care, you have little to worry about. But you need to take reasonable precautions. Your wife should eat a well-balanced diet. She should not smoke, and she should drink only in moderation. Taking drugs or medicines other than those prescribed by a doctor may be harmful.

Sometimes worries are due to superstitions, fear of the birth itself or anxiety about being a good parent. It's important for you and your wife to talk about anxieties. Prenatal classes may also help ease concerns.

38. *How can I help June deal with her fear of childbirth?*

This fear is not uncommon and can take various forms. Some women can't bear the thought of vaginal examinations. Others fear pain.

Some of these fears are understandable, others irrational. The information and advice given at prenatal classes should help put your wife at ease, both physically and psychologically. Her worries are probably due to not knowing what to expect. Talking about doubts and fears with you, her doctor and the prenatal teachers should be helpful.

Many women are less worried if they understand muscle contractions of labor have a *positive* function. Arrange to visit labor and delivery rooms with your wife before the birth. Then the surroundings will be familiar to her. You will also learn how you can help your wife during labor at prenatal classes.

39. *Mary's father just died, and she is upset. They were very close. She is now three months pregnant. Can this emotion affect our baby?*

Women used to be told to think only about beautiful things during pregnancy. They were told to keep away from anything unpleasant, because it could harm the baby.

There is a connection between emotions and physical health. We know the menstrual cycle can be upset by anxiety or stress. Shock may cause your blood pressure to drop. Certain physical changes can affect your mental state, too. Hormonal imbalance may cause severe premenstrual tension or bring on postnatal blues. The interaction is a complex one.

Severe stress to a pregnant woman may affect her unborn child to some degree. It might decrease his birth weight. It's unlikely your wife's grief will harm the baby. But tell your doctor about it so he can watch the progress of the pregnancy. Your wife will need all the emotional support you can give her.

40. *Alison is almost due and seems bored, even irritated, by the pregnancy. How can I help her through the next few weeks?*

It's not surprising she feels this way. It's a common feeling in the last few weeks of pregnancy. She probably feels uncomfortable, tired and impatient for the baby to arrive. She may have given up her job, which could lead to boredom. She may see her enlarged image as unattractive.

There are things you can do to make the last few weeks more pleasant for her. Buy her a little present. Enjoy a relaxed evening out together. Keep in mind how apprehensive she probably is. She needs you to boost her confidence.

41. *Janet says she's been having strange dreams lately. Are these common during pregnancy?*

Women often have dreams about the safety of the unborn baby. Men report having them, too. Don't be surprised if you find yourself dreaming the baby has disappeared down the drain or you forgot where you put him.

Don't take strange dreams seriously. They are a reflection of subconscious fears about your new parental role.

DISCOMFORTS OF PREGNANCY

42. *Is there anything I can do to help Alicia with her morning sickness?*

Morning sickness is normal. It's one of the most common symptoms of pregnancy. Many women experience it before pregnancy is confirmed. Some women get a vague feeling of nausea with loss of appetite. Others have more unpleasant reactions and may even lose weight. If this happens, consult your physician. He may be able to suggest help before the weight loss becomes serious.

Morning sickness usually stops by the 14th week. If it persists longer, consult your doctor.

No one knows what causes morning sickness. It is probably due to hormonal changes of pregnancy. It might be a lack of a specific vitamin.

Reassure your wife about it. Unless morning sickness is severe for a long period, your baby won't be harmed. Your wife may be worried about this aspect.

There are several things you can do to make her feel less queasy. A cup of tea with crackers or dry toast in the morning may help. She might try eating small meals often instead of having large, heavy meals. Encourage her to eat what she feels she wants.

You may notice she stops eating certain foods. Many women develop a distaste for things that are not good for them during pregnancy.

There has been controversy over some anti-nausea drugs and the side effects and possible birth defects they cause. If your doctor prescribes something to relieve the sickness, be sure there are no side effects. He may also recommend a form of vitamin B.

43. *June's face seems a little swollen. She is six months pregnant. Is it anything to worry about?*

A little swelling of the face during pregnancy is normal. Some swelling is due to additional fat deposits and fluid as the pregnancy develops. Severe swelling may be caused by pre-eclampsia. See page 9. Consult your doctor immediately if swelling is severe. He will recommend treatment.

Don't worry about a little swelling. June's face should return to normal after the birth, when she starts to lose weight.

44. *Martha's fingers are swollen, and she can't wear her wedding ring. Is this normal?*

This type of swelling is another indication of fluid retention that often occurs in pregnancy. It has been suggested the model for Leonardo da Vinci's *Mona Lisa* was pregnant. At the time the *Mona Lisa* was painted, all women of noble rank wore rings. The woman da Vinci painted wears none at all, which may indicate she had swollen fingers.

There is usually nothing to worry about with a little swelling. But if your wife's swelling persists, consult your doctor. He may recommend something to relieve the fluid retention and any discomfort.

45. *Susan has been complaining of swollen ankles. She's eight months pregnant. Is this something to worry about?*

This swelling is called *edema.* It is fairly common late in pregnancy. It's usually caused by pressure from the baby that impedes a woman's vein drainage system. This causes excess fluid in the lower body, especially the ankles and feet.

There are many things that will alleviate the condition. Plenty of rest helps. Your wife should sit with her feet up. Moving the feet in a circular motion, as well as up and down several times a day will also help. Severe swelling may indicate problems with blood pressure. Medical advice should be sought.

46. *This is the first time Paula has ever suffered from hemorrhoids. Are they common during pregnancy?*

Hemorrhoids are a form of varicose veins around the opening to the bowel. They occur frequently during pregnancy. They are usually due to partial obstruction of blood flow by pressure from the baby in the womb. Constipation, straining to empty the bowel or diarrhea can aggravate the problem.

Your wife should talk to her doctor about this problem. Fresh fruit and vegetables, in addition to bran, can help prevent constipation. During pregnancy, it's unwise to take medication for the condition without seeking medical advice.

47. *Meg says she's constipated. Is this common in pregnancy? Should she seek medical advice about it?*

Constipation during pregnancy sometimes occurs as the result of a change in hormonal action. This can make the bowel lazy. Some iron pills also have a constipating effect on some women.

Your wife's diet should contain lots of roughage. She should not push or strain a bowel movement, because it can cause hemorrhoids. She should talk to her doctor if the problem continues. She should *not* take laxatives without her doctor's advice.

48. *Is Helen's backache an inevitable part of pregnancy?*

Backache is fairly common during pregnancy. It's

Backache can cause discomfort in the later stages of pregnancy. If your wife maintains good posture and wears comfortable shoes, it should help. Consult your doctor if pain persists.

often due to hormonal changes causing discomfort in the hip area at the lower end of the pelvis. When it occurs late in pregnancy, it can be due to overweight.

The uterus may press on the front of the pelvis. The back arches and muscle strain results. There are many things to do to ease the problem. Simple remedies like a good back rub often work wonders. Some doctors recommend wearing a pregnancy girdle to give support.

A backache may also be attributed to posture. Many pregnant women stand incorrectly and put

Your active participation in exercising is helpful. Practice exercises together so they become second nature. These exercises, together with an understanding of the birth process, will help make labor easier for your wife.

strain on their backs. A woman should be encouraged to walk and stand straight. Her neck and back should be in alignment, with her bottom tucked in. She should be careful when lifting things. She should bend her knees and keep her back as straight as possible to avoid strain.

Relaxation exercises taught in prenatal classes may help prevent backache. Wearing comfortable, low-heel shoes can also help. If backache continues, your wife should talk to her doctor. Severe backache can be a symptom of other problems, such as kidney trouble or a urinary infection.

49. *Debby is four months pregnant. On a two-hour car trip, we had to stop three times for her to go to the bathroom. Is it normal for her to need to empty her bladder so often early in pregnancy?*

This is common in early pregnancy. It's basically a competition for space. Your wife's uterus is taking up more room than usual, resulting in pressure on the bladder. Routine urine tests at the doctor's office will reveal if this condition is due to other causes. The need to urinate will decrease as her pregnancy continues. The womb grows up out of the way of the bladder. This condition will occur again as the birth gets nearer and there is pressure on the bladder again.

50. *Carol has cramps in her legs, especially in bed at night. Is this common during pregnancy? Can we do anything to prevent it?*

There is nothing unusual about leg cramps during pregnancy, but they can be painful. There are many causes of cramps. Sometimes low calcium levels are the problem. Your doctor may recommend drinking more milk or taking calcium tablets.

Occasional cramps may be due to a lack of salt. This often occurs in hot weather when salt may be lost with body fluids through perspiration. More salt may need to be taken with food. Poor circulation and pressure on certain blood vessels can also cause cramps. Check with your doctor.

When your wife gets cramps, she should draw her foot up or stretch it as hard as she can. This should release the spasm. You may also be able to massage away her cramp. Your doctor may prescribe vitamin B supplements, which help in some cases.

CARING FOR MOTHER-TO-BE

51. *Daphne has a bad cold that won't go away. Is this connected to her pregnancy?*

It's often hard to get rid of a bad cold or cough after the sixth month of pregnancy. The diaphragm and chest muscles are restricted as the uterus expands. There may be a problem in clearing the breathing passages. Your wife should tell her doctor. He will be able to recommend something to help with the symptoms.

52. *Why is it important for a pregnant woman to have regular dental treatment?*

Good care of the teeth during pregnancy is important. Brushing and flossing after each meal is necessary. It used to be thought the baby took calcium from the mother's teeth. We now know this is unlikely.

During pregnancy, a woman's gums may soften as a result of hormonal action. Teeth may be more easily infected by food particles. Your wife should see her dentist regularly throughout pregnancy, and she should tell him she is expecting.

Some research indicates small amounts of fluoride taken during pregnancy help protect the developing baby's teeth. Your dentist will advise your wife about this.

53. *I've heard that X-rays can be harmful during pregnancy. Is this true?*

X-rays can be harmful to the developing child. They are usually done only late in pregnancy, when there is little risk to your baby. The radiation from multiple X-rays can damage chromosomes. Although a baby may be normal, there is evidence a form of cancer may develop in later life.

It's also important for your wife to tell her dentist she is pregnant. Dental X-rays can be harmful, too. When X-raying lower teeth, the machine is directed down toward the developing baby. X-rays may usually be done late in pregnancy without risk to the baby.

54. *Why does Molly sometimes get short of breath?*

At about 34 weeks, the baby has not dropped into the pelvis. It puts more pressure on your wife's lungs. She may find she gets breathless when she climbs the stairs or does something strenuous. This is a sign she should take things easier. After the baby moves down into the pelvis, this symptom will be less troublesome.

55. *Is it dangerous for a pregnant woman to be around someone with German measles? Should we avoid visiting my brother, whose daughter is just getting over an attack?*

German measles, also called *rubella,* is dangerous only if the pregnant woman *contracts* the disease. A blood test is done at the first prenatal visit. This will tell whether she is immune and *cannot* contract the disease. If she is immune, there is no concern about exposure. If she is not immune, she should definitely avoid exposure to a person with rubella.

Children are now vaccinated to keep them from getting rubella. If vaccinated at an older age, a woman must be sure she doesn't become pregnant for about three months. If your wife is exposed to rubella, tell your doctor immediately. It may be

A warm bath can be relaxing. Make sure the water is not too hot—hot water may cause feelings of faintness. As pregnancy progresses, you may need to help your wife in and out of the tub. Be sure there is no danger of her slipping. A shower may be better in the later stages.

possible to stop harmful effects with injections of gamma globulin.

Certain malformations of the fetus can result if German measles is contracted early in pregnancy. This is especially true during the first six weeks of pregnancy. The virus passes through the placenta and can injure the baby's ears, eyes or heart. Congenital heart disease, blindness, deafness and mental retardation can result in the fetus if the mother contracts German measles.

56. *Is it safe for Sylvia to have a daily bath during pregnancy?*

There should be no reason to alter her routine. The water should not be too hot. This may cause a feeling of dizziness. As pregnancy progresses, you might need to help her in and out of the tub. You don't want her to slip.

57. *Lucy insists it's all right for her to be driving when she's five months pregnant. Do you agree?*

Most doctors probably agree there's no reason for a woman to stop driving. Attitudes toward wearing

Your wife may continue to drive during pregnancy, depending on how confident and comfortable she feels.

seat belts in pregnancy differ. Consult your doctor about seat belts. If it's necessary for your wife to stop driving, she'll know when she should stop. Driving could be very uncomfortable.

58. *A friend said it's bad for Alice to feed our cat while she's pregnant. Is this an old wives' tale or is there truth in it?*

A parasite can be found in the feces of an infected cat. If you were infected, your symptoms would probably be mild. If a pregnant woman becomes infected, the disease can be passed through the placenta to the baby. However, such incidences are rare.

If you are anxious, take care of the pet yourself. Your wife can also wear rubber gloves when feeding the cat and removing its litter.

59. *Frances is four months pregnant. She feels sleepy a lot of the time. Is this a normal part of pregnancy?*

Yes, it often is. Frances' body is telling her to slow down, relax and adjust to her pregnancy. Encourage her to give in to the tiredness, get plenty of rest and relax more.

CHANGES IN HER BODY

60. *Jacqueline says her eyesight has changed during pregnancy. Is that normal?*

She should mention this to her doctor. Pregnancy does not usually affect the eyes. But if there is excessive fluid retention, certain changes may occur. Visual disturbances may be connected with a diabetic condition.

Your wife may find it uncomfortable to wear contact lenses during pregnancy because of fluid retention. Her eyes should return to normal after the birth.

61. *Is there anything Millie can do to avoid getting varicose veins during pregnancy?*

Varicose veins often occur during pregnancy because of extra pressure from the uterus on blood vessels or hormonal action. They can be ugly and painful. About 10% of all expectant mothers develop varicose veins, which often return to normal after birth.

There are many things you can encourage your wife to do. She should avoid standing still for too long. If she must stand, have her do a form of *isometric* exercise. Isometrics involve tightening and relaxing the knees and rocking gently from foot to foot. She can also bend and stretch her toes while sitting, watching television or talking on the telephone.

Your wife should rest during the day with her legs raised higher than the rest of her body. If varicose veins appear, she should wear support stockings or tights. A diet rich in bran may help prevent varicose veins.

62. *Sarah said she felt faint today. Is this normal in pregnancy?*

Many women feel faint at some time during early pregnancy. This is usually due to lower blood pressure. It may be due to a greater need by the uterus for blood and the effect of the hormone *progesterone*. Progesterone makes the blood flow to the lower part of the body. When blood pressure falls, the supply of oxygen to the brain is reduced. A feeling of faintness results.

Your wife can avoid feeling faint by not standing still for long periods. She should not get up too quickly after sitting. If she feels faint, she should take several deep breaths. This will help blood pressure return to normal.

63. *Is there anything Elaine can do to prevent stretch marks?*

It depends on the woman's skin and how elastic it is. Stretch marks can appear on the abdomen, buttocks and breasts as a result of skin stretching and hormonal changes. Some women's skin returns to normal after birth. Others find their skin remains stretched. It will help if your wife doesn't gain too much weight during pregnancy. Oiling and creaming the abdomen may help keep skin soft, but it won't prevent stretch marks.

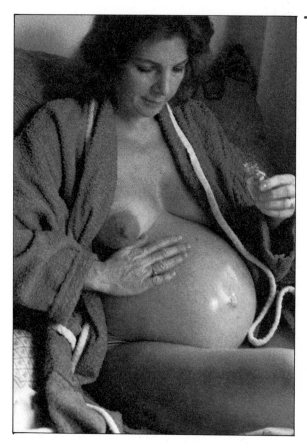

Stretch marks are common in pregnancy. You may also notice other changes in your wife's skin. The linea nigra—the line that runs down her abdomen—will fade after birth.

The dark line running down from the navel is called the *linea nigra*. It is a result of the change in hormone balance. It has nothing to do with stretch marks and lightens after your baby is born.

64. *Joan has started snoring. Could this have anything to do with her pregnancy?*

Yes, it could. During pregnancy, there is a general increase in the body's mucus secretions. As a result, your wife may have more nasal mucus. She may find it difficult to breathe through her nose normally. Your doctor may be able to give her something to relieve this. Otherwise, suggest she sleep on her side or with her head propped up. You can buy earplugs or use cotton. Don't be too concerned about this condition. She should sleep quietly again after birth.

65. *As Pauline has put on weight, her navel has begun to protrude a little. Is this normal during pregnancy?*

This often happens and is nothing to worry about. Your wife's umbilicus will return to normal after the birth of your baby.

66. *I've noticed a dark line developing down Angela's stomach. Is this normal?*

The dark line running down from the navel is called the *linea nigra.* It is one form of skin pigmentation that occurs normally in pregnancy. In very fair women, it may hardly show. It usually fades soon after birth. There are also other changes in skin pigmentations. Your wife's nipples and the *areola,* the area around them, will darken. Freckles may occur on her cheeks and forehead.

OTHER CHILDREN

67. *What is the ideal age difference between children?*

There is probably no such thing as an *ideal* age difference. It depends on your wife's health, your resources and how well you cope with other children. Research shows the popular two-year gap is difficult. It is the one most likely to lead to jealousy between siblings.

Relationships are influenced by upbringing and personalities. Sometimes jealousy takes the form of withdrawal or resentment against the parents or other child. Feelings of fondness and fear of loss of parental attention may be confused in a child's mind. Involve an older child in the care of the newborn. Spend as much time as you can with the older child, and give him affection in a way he can understand.

68. *How far in advance should we tell our 4-year-old daughter about the new baby? How can we help her adapt to the idea of a new brother or sister?*

The reality of a new arrival may cause feelings of jealousy. For four years, your daughter has had your undivided attention. However, most children are fascinated by the idea of a new baby. Start by showing her some books about babies written for children. Explain how her new brother or sister is growing inside mommy's tummy. Let her feel the movement. Visiting friends or relatives with small babies is also a good idea.

Don't tell her too much too soon. Wait until about the seventh month, or she may be bored or irritated by the idea.

You may plan for your daughter to stay with someone while your wife is in the hospital. Or someone may be coming to stay with you to help out. Plan for her care in advance so there aren't too many changes in your daughter's life all at once.

Keep her routine as close to normal as possible. This isn't the time for her to be starting a new school. Take her with you to the hospital to see mommy and the new baby if possible. Your daughter will need to be reassured she still has an important place in your affections. She is also important as an older sister.

It's better not to tell an older child about the expected new baby until late in the pregnancy. It may be appealing in the beginning, but harder to deal with later.

69. *Is it a good idea for Ann to be lifting our 3-year-old son while she's pregnant?*

You don't want to deprive your 3-year-old or your wife of contact with one another. It's a matter of how she picks him up. Encourage her to bend her knees and drop down to him. She should also squat like this when doing housework. She shouldn't bend her back.

YOUR ACTIVE
UNBORN BABY

70. *When will Claire first feel our baby moving? Will I be able to feel the baby kicking, too?*

Your wife will probably tell you the moving baby feels like gas or a bubble bursting. Movement will probably occur around 18 weeks, maybe earlier. Soon you'll be able to feel your child kick if you place your hands on your wife's abdomen.

At about 24 weeks, these movements grow stronger. You may also be able to hear your child's heartbeat through a fetal stethoscope at the doctor's office. The prospect of fatherhood becomes real when you're aware of the physical movements of your developing baby.

71. *Mary thinks our unborn child can hear because of reactions to certain sounds. Is this true?*

There is evidence an unborn child may respond to sound. This begins about the seventh month of pregnancy.

Some mothers find their unborn child gets active in response to music or loud noises. Even the sound of a typewriter starting a new line has caused movement. One researcher reported babies respond actively to musical recordings, as well as to sounds of household appliances.

Your unborn child is probably conscious of various sounds. He hears his mother's heartbeat and the gurglings of her digestive system. After the birth, you may notice your wife holds your baby on her left side. This position seems to quiet the baby, as if he's comforted by hearing his mother's heartbeat again.

The effect of the sound of the human heartbeat on

Feeling the baby move is one of the joys of a father-to-be.

infants has been tested. The infants' physical and emotional responses were observed. Most of the babies who listened to the heartbeat gained more weight than those who did not. Many of those who were not exposed to the recordings lost weight. Those who heard the heartbeat did not cry as much. The sound seemed to have a calming effect.

One toy company now makes a teddy bear with a recording of a heartbeat inside it. The recording is turned on and an infant may be calmed by the familiar rhythm. This bear can be used until the child is about 3 months old.

72. *Cynthia, who is eight months pregnant, said she thought our baby had hiccups. Could that be?*

It seems strange, but the throbbing some women experience in the lower part of the abdomen could be hiccups. These may be caused as the baby swallows some of the surrounding amniotic fluid. Your wife's instinctive feelings may be right.

73. *Is it true babies sometimes suck their thumbs while in the womb?*

This may be true. Many reflexes develop during different stages of pregnancy. Among them is the sucking reflex. The baby will need this reflex for feeding when he is born. Sucking his thumb may be practice.

74. *We have heard it's possible to stimulate our baby's senses prior to birth. Is this true?*

Research has shown your developing baby is sensitive, even before he is born. He may be capable of responding to touch, movement and even light by the seventh month of pregnancy. Premature babies prove this point. They are less-developed physically than full-term babies, but they respond to certain external stimuli.

Your baby is constantly stimulated by his mother's movements, heartbeat and breathing. Other forms of stimulation may be beneficial to his development. These things include yoga, swimming, deep-breathing exercises, music, speech and singing. If the mother's abdomen is exposed to the sun for short periods, the baby may be exposed to light.

MULTIPLE BIRTHS

75. *Freida was taking a fertility drug. What are the chances we will have a multiple birth?*

A multiple birth is not inevitable. A low percentage of women who take fertility drugs have multiple births. Chances of your wife producing triplets, or an even larger family, are remote. It is unlikely a multiple birth would be a surprise. An ultrasound scan would reveal the presence of more than one baby before the final stages of pregnancy.

76. *Twins run on Judy's side of the family. What is the chance we will have twins?*

Twins born from separate eggs, each egg fertilized by different sperm, are fraternal—not identical—twins. They are the most common form of twins. Twins may also result from the splitting of a single fertilized egg. Identical twins result. Because they are identical, these twins are always the same sex, two girls or two boys.

The incidence of producing fraternal twins at age 20 is about 3 per 1,000 births. The chance increases as the woman grows older. By age 30 it is 10 per 1,000. It continues to rise until the mother is about 38. It peaks at 16 per 1,000, then declines rapidly. At the end of the woman's fertile life, the chance of producing fraternal twins is low. The identical-twin rate at age 45 is about 4 per 1,000 births.

Tests done during pregnancy usually reveal the presence of twins. But even today, because of the way they may have been lying in the uterus, there are occasions when twins are a surprise.

77. Tests show we are expecting twins. Is there anything we should keep in mind during the pregnancy?

Your doctor will want to keep a close eye on your wife's progress. He will check the iron content of her blood. She'll need to get adequate rest to prevent high blood pressure.

Having twins is no excuse for overeating. Your wife will need to watch her weight. Twins usually have a lower birth weight than average, and they may be more frail. It is important for your wife to see her doctor regularly after 14 weeks. He will probably want to see her every two weeks. Toward the end of her pregnancy, he will see her once a week.

Twins are often delivered normally. If they are lying awkwardly, a Caesarean section may be needed.

MISCARRIAGE IN PREGNANCY

78. Stephanie had a miscarriage early in a pregnancy last year. We want things to go smoothly this time. Should she be resting most of the time?

No one knows why miscarriages occur early in a pregnancy. Ten to thirty percent of all women miscarry in the first three months. This may happen before they realize they are pregnant.

Miscarriages are not caused by anything you or your wife have done. It is important to deal with any feelings of guilt she may have about the miscarriage. Reassurance that it was *not* her fault is the most important thing you or her doctor can do.

A frank discussion with your doctor about the cause of the miscarriage is necessary. But definite answers are often not possible. To date, medical science can't prevent most miscarriages.

79. *What should we do if there seems to be a threatened miscarriage?*

Don't worry unnecessarily about it. If there are any signs of bleeding and pain, your wife should go to bed. Call the doctor immediately.

He will probably prescribe rest. He may tell you to avoid making love for a while. Your wife should not use tampons for the bleeding.

If a miscarriage seems imminent, your wife may be admitted to the hospital. If a miscarriage occurs at home, keep what is expelled for the doctor to examine. This will help him judge whether the miscarriage was complete.

If a miscarriage occurs, your wife will need your emotional support for some time. Your doctor will advise whether you should contemplate another pregnancy right away or wait.

80. *My mother-in-law had several miscarriages. Is the problem hereditary? Is Karen likely to miscarry, too?*

There is little evidence to show a tendency to miscarry is hereditary. This doesn't mean your wife *won't* miscarry. But put her mind to rest as far as any family history is concerned. Different people, different sperm and different circumstances mean you can't relate Karen's mother's experience with this pregnancy.

PREPARING FOR BIRTH

81. *I've heard a doctor may have to turn a baby so he is in the correct position to be born. What does this mean?*

Usually the baby's position changes automatically so the crown of the head is presented at birth. It may be necessary for the doctor to help the baby into this position at the end of the pregnancy. The procedure is a gentle one. The doctor moves the baby by working on the mother's abdomen from the outside. The baby may swing back to the previous position. The process may have to be repeated. It is not painful, so don't worry about it.

82. *Is it important for Helena and me to attend prenatal classes?*

You and your wife will benefit from the advice and guidance given at prenatal classes. You need to learn the exercises and techniques. If you choose natural childbirth, you will be her coach. You will meet other couples who are about to give birth.

You will both learn breathing methods to help with contractions. You'll be shown how to help your wife relieve backache, avoid exhaustion and take advantage of time between contractions. You will learn about positions your wife can use during labor to help alleviate pain. These will make the birth experience more comfortable and enjoyable.

Unprepared women often have the most difficult labors. Instinctive reactions may not be helpful. Concentration methods taught in class may help distract her from the pain of childbirth.

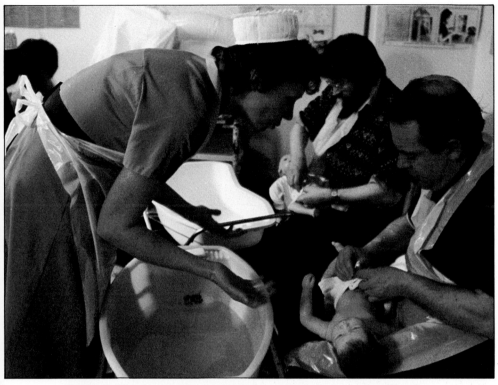
Fathers' classes can be fun and helpful, too. Many men attending the classes may also be new to fatherhood.

83. *In addition to prenatal classes, I've heard there are fathers' classes. What are these like? Do you recommend them?*

It is worthwhile to take classes that are offered. The type of classes available may vary from area to area. Sometimes it will be a one-time fathers' evening. Sometimes a series of classes is held. You will learn many things. Meeting with other expectant fathers can be enlightening and enjoyable. Shared experiences can help quell nervousness.

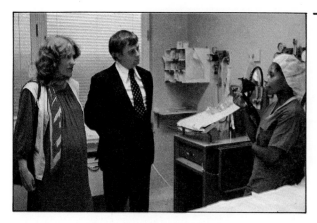

Your hospital may allow you to visit the delivery room before the birth. Someone may explain the various forms of pain relief that are available.

84. *Will it be possible for us to visit the hospital before the birth?*

Some hospitals will arrange this. A visit may be organized by the prenatal classes you attend. You may be able to visit the labor and delivery rooms. Some hospitals show movies or slides to acquaint you with their procedures.

85. *I'd like to help Dottie get her suitcase ready for the hospital. What should it contain?*

The following list is recommended for the mother-to-be:
- Two nightgowns.
- Plenty of underwear.
- A robe.
- Slippers.
- Two nursing bras.
- Clothes to go home in.

Also bring the following:

Cosmetics bag with soap, toothpaste, toothbrush, brush, comb, perfume and makeup. Books and writing materials are also useful.

For the baby, bring a nightgown and a receiving blanket. Diapers will probably be supplied by the hospital.

86. *I want to be with Abby at the birth of our first child. Will there be any problems about my being in the delivery room?*

Most hospitals encourage husband participation. You will probably be asked to leave *only* if there are complications. You may also be asked to leave if your wife has a Caesarean section under a general anesthetic.

You will be given a gown to wear in the delivery room. In some hospitals a special head covering and face covering are also provided.

87. *We can't marry before the birth of our child. Can I still go to the doctor with Valerie? Will I be allowed to be present at the birth?*

Check with your doctor to see what the hospital rules are. Many hospitals allow other family members in the delivery room, in addition to the father.

88. *I don't know if I want to be at the birth. Do you think I'll be letting Kitty down if I'm not there?*

The most common reason the husband doesn't want to be present at the birth is he feels useless. Nothing could be further from the truth. With the husband acting as coach, labor progresses more quickly and easily. The need for medication for discomfort may be reduced considerably.

Most women want their husbands with them during labor. Talk with your wife about it before the birth. She may understand how you feel, if you haven't been able to overcome your initial reaction. She may prefer to cope on her own.

Some women do *not* want their husbands with them during birth. They don't want to be seen in what they think is an undignified state.

Talk about it with your wife. Fathers who thought they wouldn't enjoy being at the birth may find it the most thrilling experience of their lives.

89. *The doctor has told Emily the baby's head is now "engaged." What does that mean?*

During the eighth month of pregnancy, a mother may feel a sensation known as the *lightening*. This occurs when the baby moves down into the pelvic girdle. Your baby's body is turned so his head is positioned to enter the birth canal. He can be felt vaginally by the doctor at this point. This doesn't mean that birth is immediately imminent, but it isn't far off. Your wife may find she is more comfortable at this point in the pregnancy.

90. *I've heard of something called the "show." What is it?*

It's one of the signs that labor may be about to begin. A *show* is the loss of a plug of mucus, sometimes with a little blood. This mucus has been plugging the cervix, the neck of the womb. It prevents infection from reaching the baby. If the show is accompanied by a heavy blood loss, or if there is bleeding without any sign of the show, contact your doctor immediately.

QUESTIONS ABOUT LABOR

91. *Jenny is only five months pregnant but says she can already feel contractions. Is it her imagination?*

The uterus does contract at various times during pregnancy. The sensation is a peculiar, but fairly painless one. Early contractions are called *Braxton-Hicks* contractions. The abdomen suddenly hardens, then within a few seconds returns to normal.

The feeling comes and goes, with no regular rhythm which indicates true contractions of labor. Early contractions may go unnoticed by some women. They are believed to aid the circulation of blood through the uterus. Braxton-Hicks contractions are not true contractions of labor.

92. *How can we be sure when labor has started? At what stage should I take Madeline to the hospital?*

First indications of labor vary from one woman to another, and from one pregnancy to another. The usual signs include contractions, which increase in frequency and strength. The breaking of the waters surrounding the baby produces a gush of warm, colorless fluid. This is also an indication.

Another sign is the appearance of the show, a plug of mucus that has sealed the cervix. It may be lost with a little blood, although this can occur days before labor actually begins, especially if an internal exam has been performed.

Call the doctor and give the approximate time of contractions. You will be told when to come to the hospital. Sometimes false alarms are due to constipation or pressure on the bowel. Always call your doctor and ask for a medical opinion.

When your wife feels labor contractions begin, time their frequency and duration. Call the doctor and give him the information. It's probably a good idea to stay close to home when the due date is near.

93. *What brings on labor, and how long will it last?*

It can happen at any time, day or night, anywhere! No one knows why labor starts spontaneously. One theory is the fetus begins to release a hormone that brings on labor. It can be induced artificially, by breaking the waters or administering certain drugs.

No one can accurately predict the length of labor. Women expecting a first child usually experience longer labor. The average duration is about 12 hours, with variations extending to over 24 hours.

94. *Is it true intercourse might cause labor to start?*

That's an old wives' tale. There is no reason you can't make love during pregnancy, unless your doctor advises against it.

Intercourse stimulates the vagina and the cervix, the neck of the womb. It might play a part in the onset of labor in some women, or it might be a coincidence. This is something we aren't certain about.

95. *Is there any way Polly can bring on labor herself if she is overdue?*

A dose of castor oil is *not* recommended. It is more likely to cause bad diarrhea. The belief that drinking alcohol will bring on labor is a dangerous myth. Your wife should be as active as possible, without getting too tired. Her doctor may consider inducing labor if she is overdue.

96. *What happens when the waters break?*

Toward the end of pregnancy, usually before labor starts, the amniotic sac bursts naturally. Fluid that has been protecting the fetus escapes through the vagina.

Some women are afraid this might happen when they are out. They dread the embarrassment of fluid suddenly gushing out of them. Put your wife at ease by telling her it doesn't usually occur obviously. The amount of fluid by the 38th week of pregnancy is about a pint. Your baby occupies a larger space in the amniotic sac. It will probably feel as if she's unable to control her bladder.

When the waters break, labor contractions usually follow. Once they start, call the doctor. He will tell you when he wants your wife to be at the hospital.

Occasionally, the waters break before the estimated date of delivery. Call your doctor immediately, and he will advise you.

When labor is induced, the membranes are ruptured by the doctor. This process is known as an *amniotomy*. It is not painful, because there are no nerves in the membranes of the amniotic sac.

OTHER QUESTIONS ABOUT PREGNANCY

97. *Rita is five months pregnant. She says I've been putting on weight, too. Could this be what I've heard called a "sympathetic pregnancy"?*

You have probably just been overeating. A true sympathetic pregnancy is rare. A recent survey into paternal reactions to pregnancy showed the following results:

- 27% of men said their wives' pregnancies had physical and psychological effects on them.
- 71% said there was no noticeable effect.

Occasionally, the medical profession has recorded instances of a man developing appendicitis just before labor begins. In one case, a man put on weight

Some fathers develop certain parallel symptoms when their wives are pregnant, such as weight gain, nervousness and nausea. This is known as a sympathetic pregnancy.

each time his daughters became pregnant.

Many men report milder symptoms. These include an inability to eat, nausea and tiredness. Whatever the reason for these symptoms, they may reflect the father's concern. As men take an increasing interest in pregnancy and birth, we may recognize these conditions as symptoms of the pregnant father.

98. *Do women really have phantom pregnancies?*

Yes, but the condition is rare. A *phantom pregnancy* is a false pregnancy. Although the pregnancy is false, it seems real to the woman experiencing it. She may have missed her period. Her breasts may have enlarged, and she may have put on weight. She is convinced she is pregnant.

If your wife has had a positive pregnancy test by her doctor, it won't be a false pregnancy. Sufferers are usually those who want a child but have failed to become pregnant. Women who have miscarried in a previous pregnancy may also have phantom pregnancies.

99. *Gwen conceived, even though she uses an intrauterine device (IUD) for contraception. Is there any danger to our child?*

Your wife should see her doctor immediately. An IUD increases the risk of a miscarriage. Some women have given birth without removal of the IUD. The device is removed only early in pregnancy. There may be an increased risk of an ectopic pregnancy with an intrauterine device. See page 7.

100. *Heather forgot to take the pill for two days and is pregnant. We are worried this may have some effect on the health of our child.*

There is no evidence birth-control pills have an effect on the developing baby.

101. *Last night Shiela woke me up, demanding strawberries and cream. I've heard of women getting certain cravings during pregnancy, but strawberries at 3 a.m.! What are cravings?*

No one knows why cravings occur during pregnancy, but there are many theories. Some say they are a sign of a dietary deficiency. Others feel

Cravings are common during pregnancy. Some women don't like foods they enjoyed. Maybe their system is warning them these substances are not good for them or the developing baby.

cravings are an unconscious attempt to satisfy an emotional need.

Whatever the cause, pregnant women may get strange cravings at times. Some women even crave things like raw meat or coal. Studies indicate desires for strange foods have occurred throughout history, within all cultures. Usually cravings disappear spontaneously. Some women also stop eating foods they love and eat foods they used to dislike. It's all normal during pregnancy.

Cravings usually disappear about the third month. Indulge your wife a little in her cravings if they don't replace a well-balanced diet.

102. *Jenny had an abortion about 10 years ago, when she was 18. Now we're expecting our first child. She was worried about whether she would be able to conceive again. Now she's anxious about whether the pregnancy and our baby will be normal.*

Discuss this together, and try to put her mind at rest. It may be a combination of guilt and unhappy memories that are making her anxious about this pregnancy. If she had good medical care, there is no evidence a single abortion results in birth problems later. If a woman has had several abortions, she should tell her doctor about these when the pregnancy is confirmed.

103. *Why are some babies born prematurely?*

The definition of a *premature baby* is a baby born after the 20th and before the 37th week of pregnancy. It weighs less than 5-1/2 pounds at birth. Between 5 and 10% of all births are premature.

There are many reasons why a baby may be born early. Some may not have been well-nourished in the womb, due to malfunctioning of the placenta. The mother may have developed toxemia or have uncontrolled diabetes. In multiple pregnancies, labor may begin early. Twins may be born at low birth weight.

In general, better standards of prenatal care have brought about a lower incidence of premature birth.

104. *Holly is blond, with blue eyes. I have darker hair and brown eyes. Which features is our baby most likely to inherit?*

Most parents-to-be spend a lot of time wondering what their baby will look like. This depends on the factors of the 23 chromosomes of the sperm and egg.

Every detail of a baby's makeup and appearance are determined at conception. These are changed only by certain aspects of environment and experiences.

Every sperm and egg have a slightly different genetic program. The possible combinations are enormous. If you were both blond, with blue eyes, you would probably produce a blond, blue-eyed child. In your case, there is only a 1-in-4 chance of your baby having blue eyes. Genes for brown eyes are *dominant*, which means they are more likely to prevail.

Women usually have darker eye coloring than men. Dark-eyed girls are in evidence and so are blue-eyed boys. Recessive genes, which are not dominant, also play a part, and there are surprises. Red hair may be inherited from a grandparent or great-grandparent, even though both parents may have different hair coloring.

Most babies are born with blue eyes. The color usually changes during the first year of life.

105. *Before we married, Julie joked she was looking for someone tall, dark, handsome and rich. He also had to be Rh-negative! Her blood group is Rh-negative and I'm Rh-positive. Is there any danger to our unborn child?*

With modern obstetric techniques, it is less of a concern. It's good to know what Rh incompatibility is. If a woman doesn't have the Rh-factor, she is Rh-negative. About 17% of the female population is Rh-negative.

Your wife may have heard if she had a baby with an Rh-positive man, the baby could be born Rh-negative or positive. If a baby is Rh-positive in a first pregnancy, it isn't relevant. Everything would proceed normally. With a second or subsequent pregnancy, some of the baby's Rh-positive blood could get into the mother's system. Rh-antibodies, set up to destroy the invading blood cells, could pass through the placenta and enter the baby's circulation. It could cause anemia and jaundice in your child.

However, there is no need to worry. An Rh-negative mother is usually given a special anti-Rh injection after the birth of her first baby. This prevents antibodies from being formed.

Even if the baby is affected, it's possible to give a blood transfusion in small quantities after birth. This can even be done while the baby is still in the uterus. This is why the blood tests given to every pregnant woman early in pregnancy are so important.

106. *I'd like to make our home babyproof. What do I need to do?*

It will be some time before the baby crawls around and gets into mischief. But there is no harm in checking on certain things now. Keep these things in mind:

- Be sure windows close securely. Bars may be advisable so a child can't fall out. Bars shouldn't be spaced so he gets his head stuck.
- Use a gate on stairs.
- Put your medicine chest up as high as possible, and be sure it locks. Keep medicines in childproof containers.
- Place guards or screens in front of gas, electric or open fires.
- Keep the balcony door locked, if you have one.
- Don't place objects that could attract a baby's attention directly above a fire.
- Make sure carpeting on the stairs is secured. Loose carpet could be dangerous when you are carrying the baby downstairs.

- Don't leave a loose rug at the bottom of stairs. You might slip while carrying the baby.
- Fit safety covers over electrical sockets so your baby can't stick his fingers in them.
- Store all plastic bags out of reach. If a baby pulls one over his head, he could suffocate.
- Put safety glass in any area where your baby may play. Safety film for covering glass is available. You can highlight glass panels with colored tape or decals.
- Label and keep all poisons, such as bleach, weed killer, disinfectant and paint thinner, where a baby can't get them. Keep the cabinet locked.
- Be sure toys are safe and non-toxic. Read labels to see if they meet U.S. Consumer Product Safety Commission and Canadian Product Safety Branch standards.
- Get in the habit of turning all pot and skillet handles inward from the edge of the stove. Be sure your baby is in his crib, highchair or playpen when you're cooking.
- Never use a hot utensil while handling baby.

107. *Will the time of year when our child is born have any effect on his character and intelligence?*

Followers of astrology might have strong opinions on this. Some have tried to plan conception so their baby will be born under a particular sign. Most doctors would agree heredity and environmental influences play a more-important part.

There is evidence a relationship exists between diet, the season a child is conceived and brain development. Researchers found after a hot summer, more mentally defective children were born the following winter and spring. This may have occurred because the pregnant women ate less. We often eat less in hot weather.

A pregnant woman needs to eat a well-balanced diet, even when it's hot. This is true during the second and third months of pregnancy, when brain development is most active. Protein intake at this time is believed to be vital. If it's hot and your wife feels salads are adequate, she should add meat, fish, cheese or eggs to her daily diet.

108. *I was a large baby, weighing 10 pounds at birth. Does that mean we'll have a large baby, too?*

Average birth weight is 7 pounds, and boys are usually heavier than girls. Even though *you* were a large baby, it will have little effect on the size of your child at birth.

Small women give birth to smaller babies. Older mothers often produce bigger babies than younger mothers. Diabetic women also produce large babies. Mothers with high blood pressure and certain kidney conditions may produce smaller babies.

The developing baby acts like a parasite. It takes what it needs from its mother, so your wife should eat a sensible diet. A well-balanced diet is important to a woman's own health during pregnancy. The baby takes all its nourishment from her system.

If a woman continues to smoke during pregnancy, the baby's birth weight may be decreased. Heavy smoking may affect the blood and oxygen supply to the uterus. This could lead to retardation.

109. *I heard the doctor refer to Annie as an "older primigravida." What did he mean?*

This is the medical term used to indicate a mother is over 30 years old and having her first child. Early prenatal care is advisable for women over 30. They often experience a longer labor, too. Statistics show there is more chance of a mother having twins when she is over 30. Caesarean sections are also more frequent.

110. *Elga is losing a lot of hair. Why?*

This sometimes happens in pregnancy. No one knows why, but it may be due to hormonal changes. We all lose some hair every day. Pregnancy speeds this up. The hair breaks or comes out at the roots. Loss should return to normal after the birth.

Most women don't experience problems with their hair. If your wife's hair is long, it may be stronger and thicker if cut to a shorter length. It may also be easier to manage. Some women find dry hair gets drier and greasy hair gets greasier during pregnancy.

Hair loss may be associated with anemia during and after pregnancy. Make sure your wife is taking her iron pills, if they were prescribed.

111. *Cleo is now six months pregnant. She wants to continue working for another two months. Is this advisable?*

This decision depends entirely on the woman, if she has a normal pregnancy. The decision she makes, if unforced, will probably be the best one. She needs accurate, appropriate information about herself, her pregnancy and her job. Then she will be in the best position to decide how long to work.

112. *I'm afraid I'll hurt the baby when we make love. Could that happen? How safe is it to continue sex during pregnancy?*

If the mother isn't uncomfortable, it should be safe to continue sexual intercourse during pregnancy.

Toward the end of the pregnancy, intercourse may be uncomfortable for your wife.

There is no scientific evidence to prove abstaining from sexual intercourse helps prevent miscarriage. You will probably be advised to abstain from intercourse if there is a threatened miscarriage.

Some men say they experience greater emotional satisfaction making love with their wives during pregnancy. For many, pregnancy provides a special opportunity for experimentation in lovemaking. It also removes any worry about contraception. Toward the end of pregnancy, a change of position and limited penetration may be more comfortable for your wife.

This is a time for great understanding on your part. Your wife may feel unattractive during pregnancy and be unable to concentrate on lovemaking. Help her maintain a positive body image, in spite of the physical and emotional changes going on. You may find her new shape and the prospect of the new life inside it thrilling. Don't forget to tell her so. There are many ways to express your feelings.

113. *Can you tell me about the dangers of sexually transmitted diseases in pregnancy?*

It is important to distinguish between various conditions and the way they can affect the unborn baby.

Non-Specific Urethritis—This disease can cause discomfort to men when they urinate. It's believed to be caused by a bacteria, but it will not disrupt a pregnancy's normal course.

Gonorrhea—This is another sexually transmitted disease. It produces an unpleasant discharge in men, but may be symptomless in women. It can be passed to a baby while he is being born. This disease causes an eye infection that may lead to blindness unless recognized and treated. If left untreated in women, gonorrhea damages tissues and blocks Fallopian tubes. Infertility may result. If it is cured, it should not disrupt a pregnancy's normal course.

Syphilis—Women are given a routine blood test early in pregnancy to check for syphilis. Early testing is vital, because syphilis is often hard to detect in women. It is less painful and has less-obvious symptoms than in a man. If detected early enough in pregnancy, it may be cured without affecting the baby. If left until later, the child may be born with syphilis. This requires immediate attention. Death may occur if the condition is left untreated.

If you or your wife fear you may have syphilis or gonorrhea, consult your doctor at once. Your unborn child may be at risk.

Genital Herpes—Now more common as a sexually transmitted disease is genital herpes. The neck of the womb or external sexual parts may have herpes spots or ulcers. The baby may be in danger if born vaginally, so a Caesarean section is often performed.

114. *Celia doesn't wear a bra. We're wondering whether she should wear one during pregnancy.*

It's advisable for women to wear a good support bra during pregnancy. As the breasts enlarge and get heavier, the bra prevents sagging. If your wife has large breasts, she may want to wear a bra day *and* night. She may wear the bra beginning early in pregnancy. Some women experience considerable growth of breasts even during the first few months.

With a bra on, have your wife measure the distance between the notch at the top of the breastbone and the nipple. She should keep this measurement the same with an adjustable bra.

She should wear a good, supportive nursing bra if she breast-feeds. It will help her regain her previous bosom size and shape more quickly.

115. *Are flat shoes best during pregnancy? Aileen seems to walk awkwardly on her heels.*

Flat shoes could cause her to put excessive weight on her heels. A broad heel, 1 to 2 inches high, is probably best. Shoes should be wide enough to give adequate support.

116. *Linda and I like to soak in our hot tub, but we've heard this can be dangerous.*

Medical authorities disagree on the effects soaking in a spa or tub has on pregnant women. Studies have shown spa and tub use can result in *hyperthermia*, or overheating of the body. In pregnant women, this condition can decrease blood flow to the fetus. If the pregnancy is complicated, it can threaten the fetus. Another potential problem with spa and hot-tub use is the spread of organisms that may cause vaginal infections.

Many doctors advise their patients not to use spas or tubs during pregnancy. Others may recommend safe water temperatures and soaking periods. In all cases, check with your doctor before using a spa or hot tub.

117. *We had planned a vacation when we found out Carol was pregnant. How safe is it for her to fly at six months?*

It's a matter of common sense. If the pregnancy is progressing normally, it is probably safe for her to fly. Consult your doctor before making any final decision. He knows your wife's medical history and can guide you toward a decision. Some airlines do not like to carry women at the end of their pregnancies.

118. *Is there evidence to show the age of the father can affect the development of the fetus?*

This is a complex area, and only a small amount of research has been done. Some studies seem to indicate there may be an increased risk of handicap if the father is over 50.

119. *Carolyn is diabetic and expecting our first child. Are there any difficulties we may encounter? Will our baby be diabetic?*

Heredity plays a part in the development of diabetes. But a baby is more likely to be diabetic if *both* parents are diabetic. Don't worry too much about this.

Your wife should give her doctor full details about her medical history. He will advise her how to control her diabetes during pregnancy. A woman's predisposition to diabetes is often triggered by factors such as diet, overweight and stress.

Before the discovery of insulin, the incidence of fertility among diabetic women was low. Today, it's almost normal, with proper control. There's no reason why your wife shouldn't have a good pregnancy.

Diabetes in a pregnant woman means close supervision of her pregnancy. This involves careful insulin control and the effect of morning sickness on insulin needs. Your wife's insulin requirement may be altered during pregnancy. This is why the diabetic woman needs regular urine and blood tests.

Your wife may have a large baby. Babies born to diabetic mothers are often large. They are sometimes delivered early, following induction or by Caesarean section.

Pregnancy may unmask a latent, but mild, incidence of diabetes. It may disappear spontaneously after the baby's birth.

120. *Abby is worried she won't be able to breast-feed because her nipples are not prominent. Is there anything we can do about this?*

Before your wife starts to worry unnecessarily, get your doctor's opinion. He will tell your wife if this is a problem and what to do.

121. *How well-protected is our baby in the womb? Will a bump disturb or damage him in any way?*

Your baby is floating in the fluid of the amniotic sac. He is well-cushioned because the fluid acts as a shock absorber. Your wife's uterine and abdominal muscles, as well as other tissues, also act as protection. Take precautions to keep her from falling or being jolted unnecessarily.

122. *Yesterday the doctor confirmed Anne is pregnant. This morning she told me she had noticed a very slight loss of blood. What should we do?*

Report any loss of blood during pregnancy to the doctor. At this stage of pregnancy, if it's only a slight loss and brown color, don't worry too much. If it's red and fairly heavy, accompanied by pain, inform your doctor immediately. It could be due to a polyp or erosion of the tissue of the cervix. This won't endanger the pregnancy. Bleeding can be a sign of threatened miscarriage.

The Birth

Childbirth has been described as a beautiful climax to a loving relationship. Holding your newborn child for the first time is one of the most rewarding moments of your life. It's even more rewarding if you have shared this experience with your wife.

As a new father, your emotions will cover a wide span. You may wonder at the miracle of life. You may feel more protective toward your wife than ever before. You will be proud of the virility that has brought you this child.

This section will help you learn about the birth process and what it will be like. It will help prepare you for this wonderful experience.

PREPARING FOR BIRTH

1. *The estimated date of delivery has come and gone. Now, four days later, we are wondering if something could be wrong.*

Don't be overanxious. Doctors allow a margin for error in calculating the estimated date of delivery. Four days is not an undue delay. Your doctor will probably want to examine your wife to decide whether induction is advisable.

2. *The doctor has suggested inducing the birth of our child. Why? Will it be uncomfortable for Sue?*

Induction is the artificial bringing on of labor. Sometimes help is necessary to get things started. It may be necessary if the baby is overdue and the placenta is failing. The mother may have high blood pressure, sometimes a symptom of pre-eclampsic toxemia. This can be a dangerous condition if left untreated. The mother may be ill or have diabetes.

Usually induction is only done between the 36th and 40th weeks of pregnancy, or later if the baby is overdue. The doctor will check carefully to see if the baby is mature and the cervix ripened and soft. Inducing labor should always benefit the mother and baby. Induction is not recommended unless necessary for *medical* reasons.

The methods of inducing labor may vary. The waters of the amniotic sac may be ruptured, which is painless. Your wife will feel a gush of tepid liquid from her vagina. Then an *oxytocin* or *Pitocin* intravenous (I.V.) drip may be started to stimulate contractions. A normal delivery usually follows. Less frequently, a Caesarean section may be performed.

3. *We have been told our baby is in the breech position. What does this mean?*

Babies are usually born head first. Doctors call this the *cephalic presentation.* However, in about 3 in every 100 births, the baby does not turn down into this position in the 30th to 34th week of pregnancy. His head is not engaged in the pelvis. It remains under his mother's ribs, even though the doctor may have attempted to turn him. This is the *breech position.* Your baby is positioned to be born bottom first.

There is no great cause for concern. Whether or not your wife has a vaginal delivery depends on the size of her pelvis. There are several alternatives. Sometimes the doctor will perform a Caesarean section. He may give epidural anesthesia or do an episiotomy to facilitate vaginal delivery. With twins, the chances are at least one will be a breech delivery.

AT THE HOSPITAL

4. *What will happen when we get to the hospital?*

A nurse will check to see if labor has started. She will ask your wife for an accurate description of her contractions. Your wife's blood pressure and pulse will be taken. Urine samples and blood samples will also be taken.

The fetal position will be checked through the abdominal wall. The nurse may listen to the baby's heart. An internal examination may be done to check the degree the cervix has already dilated.

If your wife is given a hospital gown to put on for the delivery, have her tie it in the front. This will make it easier to put the baby on her abdomen or to breast-feed immediately after birth.

5. *Will Carol's pubic hair have to be shaved before the birth?*

At one time, almost all women had their pubic hair shaved before birth. The belief was pubic hair might harbor infection and endanger the baby. People thought body hair contained germs.

Today, most hospitals only shave or clip a woman's pubic hair in the area immediately around the birth opening. There is a valid reason for this. It is done so stitches do not become entangled in the hair. That can be very painful. Shaving is done in a few seconds and doesn't hurt.

6. *Will Janet be given an enema before birth?*

Practice varies, but an enema is usually given. This empties the bowels before labor has progressed too far. There are two purposes for an enema. First, a full bowel may put undue pressure on the birth canal. This limits the space through which your baby will pass. Second, it keeps accidental bowel movements from occuring during delivery.

An enema is not painful, but it may be uncomfortable. It takes effect quickly. Suppositories containing a laxative are sometimes used. These do not work as quickly, but some women find them less unpleasant.

7. *Could you tell me something about the methods of monitoring during birth?*

The frequency and strength of contractions during labor can be measured in various ways. The nurse may do this by placing her hand on the abdomen. An electronic fetal-monitoring machine may also be used to show the pressure of the uterus during a contraction. It can show when the next one is about to start before it is felt.

A printout or screen shows the fetal heart rate. Monitoring can be done by a device strapped to the mother's abdominal wall or internally, through the vagina. Some systems of monitoring use sound waves. This involves less machinery and allows the mother to walk around.

In some hospitals, monitoring is routine. In others, it is used only in high-risk pregnancies or when labor is being induced or accelerated. Don't assume something is wrong if a monitoring system is used.

8. *I have heard some hospitals do not allow a mother to use the position she finds most comfortable for birth. Is lying on your back the best position for delivery?*

In some primitive cultures, women stand, crouch

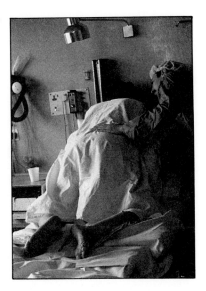

The expectant father doesn't always pace the floor outside the delivery room. He may be with his wife, helping and encouraging her with breathing techniques and easing labor with massage.

or squat while giving birth. These women seem to give birth more easily.

Some doctors permit a woman to use any position she finds comfortable. It may be easier for the doctor to check how labor is progressing if she is lying down. But other positions may be more comfortable for mother and baby.

Most mothers find it comfortable to be mobile during labor. The cervix dilates more efficiently when the mother is upright. The laws of gravity suggest the mother's task must be more difficult for her if she is lying down. It was not common practice to lie down to give birth until the 19th century.

It will be a matter of the practice preferred by your doctor, as well as what is advisable for your wife. There could be strong reasons for a woman to be lying down to give birth.

ABOUT THE BABY

9. *What is fetal distress?*

Your baby may travel only a few inches to be born, but it is one of the most hazardous journeys he will make. Most births are trouble free, but sometimes a baby's oxygen supply may be diminished. His heart rate increases, then gets irregular and drops. Lack of oxygen can be dangerous, and brain damage may result.

A monitor may be attached to your wife during labor. The length and timing of her contractions and the baby's heart rate can be recorded. In this way, fetal distress can be detected.

If there is fetal distress, rapid action may need to be taken. Usually a Caesarean section or forceps delivery will be necessary.

Don't assume because a fetal monitor is being used that there is something wrong. It's usually the doctor's way of making sure things are proceeding normally.

10. *What will our baby look like when he is born?*

He won't look his best, after his long, tiring journey. He will be damp and sticky, and a little purple, until he has his first breath of air. His head may be an odd shape because of pressure in the birth canal. The head soon becomes round. Genitals are large, compared to the rest of the body, but this is natural. He may be smaller and more frail than you had expected, and his skin will look wrinkled. He may be smeared with some blood and covered with *vernix*, a creamy, white protective substance.

He'll get better looking. To you and your wife, he's probably the most beautiful baby ever born.

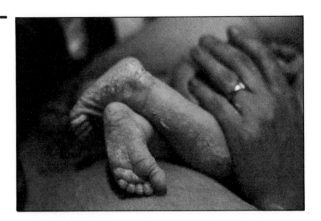

Your baby may be born covered with a creamy substance called vernix. This protects his skin while he's in the womb. Vernix is gradually absorbed by the skin and may only need to be washed from his head.

11. *Why are some babies born with a creamy white substance covering their bodies?*

This greasy, water-repellent substance is called *vernix* and is a natural barrier cream. Your baby has been living in a liquid environment for the last 9 months. During this time, vernix has protected his skin. Vernix makes newborn babies slippery and difficult to handle.

Many believe vernix may have a function in preventing skin infections. To preserve this natural barrier cream, a baby is not always bathed immediately after birth.

PAIN RELIEF

12. *Can you tell me about the different pain-relieving drugs and anesthetics Sue may be offered during labor? Will she need them?*

The pain-reliever your wife has during labor should be a personal choice, combined with advice from the doctor. Your understanding about what is involved in each method and possible side effects will help in this decision.

Natural childbirth is not for everyone. There are many methods of pain relief available to your wife if she needs them. *Demerol* is a narcotic analgesic. It may be injected into the hip or an I.V. It can affect the baby, too, although this is uncommon.

Lumbar and caudal *epidurals* freeze the mother from the waist down. She feels no pain at all. Loss of sensation also means loss of the urge to push. The mother may not experience the feeling of the baby being born.

The *paracervical block* is a local anesthetic for the first stage of labor. It is not widely used now. A *pudedal block* is used with a forceps delivery and has immediate effect.

No one will permit your wife to suffer. Reassure her that she has not failed if she needs help. If she is in great discomfort, the baby may find the journey more uncomfortable.

13. *The hospital where our child will be born offers epidural anesthesia. What is involved?*

Epidural anesthesia is not a general anesthetic involving loss of consciousness. Medication is administered in the spinal region to relieve pain by totally numbing the mother from the abdomen down. In many hospitals, it's routine, but an epidural is not available everywhere.

An epidural can provide completely pain-free childbirth. It may be ideal for a painful or long labor. There are contraindications and possible side effects. It is not advisable when there are certain neurological and skin conditions. If there is *supine hypotension,* a fall of blood pressure when lying on the back, it may not be advisable. Side effects may include nausea and a lowering of blood pressure. There may be risk of severe headache if the membrane surrounding the spinal cord is punctured.

Some women are frightened by the loss of all sensation in their legs. The mother loses her urge to push. She may require a catheter in her bladder because of this loss of feeling.

There are two types of epidural—*lumbar* and *caudal.* In both, a local anesthetic is given outside the covering of the spinal cord. A fine needle is inserted between the vertebrae in the space between the covering of the spinal cord and the bone. This is called the *epidural space.* A fine tube is pushed through the needle. The needle is withdrawn, so only the tube remains. A local anesthetic passes through the tube into the space. Further doses can be administered when the initial effect starts to wear off.

Lumbar and caudal epidurals are similar, but use different approaches to the same epidural space. Only an anesthetist skilled in the technique is allowed to administer epidural anesthesia.

Caesarean sections are also performed under epidural anesthesia. The mother remains awake during the procedure and the father may be allowed to be present.

14. *I have heard that acupuncture may be used to relieve pain during labor. Is that true?*

Acupuncture is used in China to relieve pain during labor. But it's not usually available in hospitals here, unless by special arrangement. If your doctor is interested in acupuncture, you could make inquiries about an acupuncturist in attendance at the birth. It's up to the hospital whether they agree to this. Your wife will need some experience with acupuncture before the birth.

Some claim acupuncture may improve a mother's health during pregnancy by reducing backache and swollen ankles. It may also shorten the length of labor. Fine needles are inserted in various parts of the body. These are stimulated by the acupuncturist at intervals.

Few doctors use acupuncture as a method of anesthesia. It's unlikely any could guarantee a pain-free birth. The degree of relief depends on the mother's physical and mental state.

15. *Is it true that hypnosis may be used as a form of pain relief during labor?*

Yes, hypnosis can be used as pain relief, but it rarely is. Most women prefer to be awake during labor, actively contributing in the birth process. Hypnosis works only if the subject is willing to be "put under" and is receptive to it.

When it's used, mothers are taught to hypnotize themselves. They lie comfortably in a quiet atmosphere. The hypnotist suggests to them they are in a relaxed state and even sleeping. The mothers are told about labor while in this state of suggestibility. It is suggested birth can be pain free. If this method is interesting to your wife, ask your doctor if there are facilities for instruction in your area.

16. *Is there such a thing as painless childbirth?*

Most women need help of some kind to cope with painful contractions, especially later in labor. Controlled breathing and relaxation techniques may not be sufficient. You may hear stories of women who claim to have given birth without feeling discomfort. But instances of this are extremely rare.

LABOR

17. *How long will Rachel be in labor?*

This varies from woman to woman, and from pregnancy to pregnancy. The labor experienced with a second child is usually shorter than the first. Once, a woman was allowed to labor for days. Today, the doctor will probably intervene if labor lasts longer than 24 hours. An I.V. of oxytocin may be started to stimulate the uterus to contract so labor is shortened.

18. *Is it true woman who have good prenatal instruction have shorter labors?*

A relaxed woman who is aware and understands what is going on may have a less-complicated, shorter labor. She may also need less anesthetics or pain-relieving drugs. The baby will probably find birth easier, too.

19. *I've heard there are various massages that may help during labor. Will it help Margaret if we practice these together?*

You and your wife may learn about massage for labor at prenatal classes. You will be able to help her with some. It can be comforting, but be sure your wife finds it relaxing and isn't irritated by it.

Firm, slow massage above and on either side of the lower back can give relief. You may need some oil or talcum powder to avoid skin irritation. Your wife may also find it helpful to massage the abdomen during a contraction. Using both hands, she should start down low. She should draw her hands apart, toward the hips, then up to the top of the uterus. She can also use one hand, working down one side of the abdomen, then across and up the other side. Firm pressure above and on either side of the buttocks may be helpful.

20. Why are breathing techniques important during labor?

Controlled, rhythmic breathing is one of the techniques of natural childbirth. It is helpful during labor. Some people claim 30 to 50% of the mothers who use controlled breathing do not need other pain relief.

Breathing distracts a mother from pain by not allowing her to become tense. Breathing should aid each contraction as a step toward the birth.

The techniques taught vary from one prenatal class to another. Your wife will probably be taught three levels of breathing. She will learn milder contractions require lower levels. If you are with her at the birth, encourage her to remain at the lower level of breathing for as long as she can.

Later in the first stage of labor, when contractions are more frequent and stronger, she will change to quicker, more shallow breathing. Emphasis will be on breathing out. This is the second level of breathing. Shallow breathing followed by blowing, like extinguishing a match, is the third level.

Mothers may find the rhythm of breathing changes automatically with the strength of contractions. Concentration on breathing helps divert attention from the pain. This raises the pain threshold.

21. Can you tell me about the various stages of labor?

An average labor lasts about 10 to 12 hours in a first pregnancy, and up to seven hours in subsequent pregnancies. It is never possible to anticipate its duration.

There are three stages of labor, four if you count the transition between the first and second stages. The *first stage* lasts from the onset of contractions to full dilation of the cervix.

During all stages of labor, the nurse may want to listen to the baby's heartbeat. You may be allowed to do this, too. With each contraction there is a pull on the cervix until it dilates to about 8 centimeters. The *transition stage* follows. Any vomiting that occurs now may be due to tiredness because of a low-sugar level or dehydration. A glucose I.V. may be started at this time.

In the *second stage* your wife will probably need your help. This stage is shorter. In a first pregnancy, it often lasts about 40 minutes. In subsequent pregnancies, it may last only 20 minutes. The baby's head is in the upper vagina. Your wife will need to pant to restrain the pushing urge until the doctor tells her to bear down. The cervix may not be fully dilated yet. Pushing too soon may cause it to swell, resulting in an obstruction.

Hold your wife and breathe with her. The baby's head will start to emerge with every push, until it is finally out. The crown of the head is usually up, so the baby is face-down. His head will then rotate. One shoulder will be born, then the other. The rest of his body will slide out rapidly.

The *third stage* of labor must still take place. This is the birth of the placenta. This usually follows in a few minutes. It emerges so easily your wife may not even notice it.

22. *How will I be able to help Julie during labor?*

There are many ways you'll be able to help her. Your presence at the birth will reaffirm your emotional bond. In the hospital, she will be in unfamiliar surroundings. It is helpful to have you there with her. She won't feel so vulnerable. No woman should be left alone during labor. Stay with her and give her your loving support.

Talk to her, tell her she is doing fine and you are confident she will do well. Maintain eye contact and smile at her.

Your baby may be able to sense anxiety. The birth process could become more difficult if your wife is tense. Encourage her to talk to your baby while he is being born. It may be helpful.

If you attend prenatal classes, you'll know how to help with breathing and relaxation techniques. Your wife should be in a comfortable position. You should work together during each contraction, and breathe with her. She will appreciate being freshened between contractions, too. Sponge her brow, comb her hair, encourage her to relax between contractions. Try not to get distracted by anything else going on. This may make her tense.

Tell her when you first see the baby's head emerging. The doctor may give you a mirror to hold so your wife can see the baby emerging.

Don't be surprised if you find her getting upset with you during the birth, even criticizing you. Some women react this way during labor. Sometimes it's the effect of pain-relieving drugs, sometimes it's just stress.

23. *What do you recommend for easing backache during labor?*

Backache experienced in labor is usually due to pressure from the baby's head. A position change may encourage the head into the birth canal where it won't press the small of the back. Kneeling, squatting and getting on all fours can be helpful.

A hot-water bottle can also be a good remedy. Pelvic rocking; moving the lower part of the body left to right or backward and forward, can help.

At prenatal classes, you may have learned to massage the muscles of the upper buttocks with the palms of the hands. Certain pressure points on the ball of each foot, below the central point, may relieve back pain associated with labor.

24. *What are labor pains like?*

Labor contractions are different from those that occur earlier in pregnancy, the *Braxton-Hicks contractions.* Labor contractions have a definite rhythm, causing varying degrees of discomfort. Rest periods between them gradually decrease.

No one knows what causes the discomfort. It may be the tensing and relaxing of the muscles of the womb, helping the baby proceed along the birth canal. Others say we are conditioned to expect pain in labor. Fear causes tension, resulting in pain.

At first, contractions are weak. They last for 20 to 30 seconds. Some women say the abdomen feels stiff. Others compare the sensation to a stomachache, backache or cramps.

By the end of the first stage of labor, contractions become more intense. The intervals between them decrease and they last longer. Contractions feel like a wide belt around your stomach being tightened firmly, then loosened.

Contractions come in waves, and they have a positive function. It's believed if a woman is encouraged to see this positive function, she will experience less pain.

You probably don't have to call the doctor until contractions are occurring about every five minutes. If in doubt, call earlier.

25. *Will Cindy be able to eat and drink during labor?*

In the earliest stage of labor, your wife may be able to have clear liquids. This is up to the doctor. After one hour of contractions 5 minutes apart, it's not a good idea for her to eat, in case general anesthesia is necessary.

The digestive system does not work normally during labor. This is probably because the body needs to conserve all its energy for the birth.

Water is usually not denied. If labor is prolonged or the mother is weary, she may be fed with an I.V. of glucose solution.

26. *Why is an I.V. sometimes set up in labor?*

Don't be disturbed if you see an I.V. being put up for your wife. If you have any questions, ask your doctor about it.

Your wife may benefit from a glucose solution if labor is prolonged. This keeps her from dehydrating. The I.V. allows fluid to enter her bloodstream directly through a vein in her arm. Other substances can also be introduced by the same route if necessary.

27. *Ann is afraid she'll make a fool of herself during labor and lose control.*

She shouldn't worry because the nurses are used to the behavior of women in labor. Some women say incredible things when given some methods of pain relief. If you help her with breathing and relaxation techniques, she'll be less likely to panic.

28. *Sandy is anxious she may not be able to stand the pain of labor.*

We all have different pain thresholds, due to our

emotional stability, the degree of fear we experience and our pain threshold. If your wife has had good prenatal care, she will have learned how to breathe and relax.

The period of discomfort occupies a short proportion of the whole labor. Your wife should use the rest periods between contractions wisely. Encourage her to regard pain as having a positive function. Your presence should help give her the emotional support she needs.

Some form of mental activity, such as rhythmic finger tapping, may help keep her calm during contractions. If she continues to feel overanxious, remind her there are methods of pain relief available. The doctor will not allow her to suffer.

29. Laurie is expecting twins. Will her labor be different?

Your wife will probably give birth normally. The baby in the lower position is born first. The period of time between the births may vary from a few minutes to an hour. A longer gap can occur.

Contractions start again before the second baby is born. One baby may be in a breech position. Whether there are two separate placentas or only one depends on whether there are fraternal or identical twins.

30. Will Joan get exhausted during labor? How can she avoid excessive fatigue?

Labor can be tiring. Encourage your wife to use the breathing techniques she learned and to rest between contractions. Then labor shouldn't exhaust her. Understanding the nature of childbirth should also help. It is less tiring to accomplish something you comprehend. Birth is not a test of endurance.

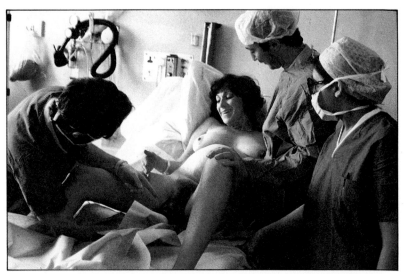

One more push and the baby's head is born. His body follows easily. He may be placed on his mother's abdomen immediately after the birth.

THE BIRTH

31. *Gloria is wondering whether she will have an episiotomy. What is involved? Why do some women have them and some not?*

An *episiotomy* involves an incision at the lower part of the vaginal opening, toward the bowel opening. It is done for the following reasons:
- To ease delivery of the baby's head.
- To prevent tearing that may be ragged and difficult to repair.
- To avoid overstretching or tearing the *perineum,* the area between a woman's vulva and anus.

There is no need for your wife to fear an episiotomy. It is painless because a local anesthetic is given. She will probably be numb in the area because of the pressure exerted on her nerves by the baby's head.

An episiotomy will be done if necessary. It won't be done if it's not needed. It may be necessary when forceps are used or with a breech birth. It's almost routine with first babies in some hospitals. There is disagreement in the medical profession as to whether it should be performed at all births.

If your wife has an episiotomy, she will have stitches. Discomfort should disappear when the stitches dissolve. Some say an episiotomy helps keep a woman's muscles in good condition.

Women who have had an episiotomy sometimes experience pain when making love for a short time afterward. You will need to be careful and gentle.

32. We have heard we should avoid a forceps delivery. What is involved? Why should it be necessary?

Forceps are like large tongs. They are used to ease out the baby's head during delivery. Forceps come in many shapes and designs, according to the situation they are used for.

You may be anxious about forceps damaging your baby. Forceps are so efficient as instruments that it is unlikely any harm could occur. They are used only for the baby's benefit. These include when the baby is having a hard time coming out or he is in a breech position or other difficult presentation. They may be used if there is some sign the baby or mother is in distress.

The fears you express probably remain from the time when forceps were used in situations where a Caesarean is more likely today. Their use may be recommended to protect the head during delivery.

Forceps may be used if the mother has epidural anesthesia. Her natural urge to push cannot be felt in the second stage. Anesthesia is usually given if forceps are used. There is no pain felt at their insertion. An episiotomy to widen the birth opening

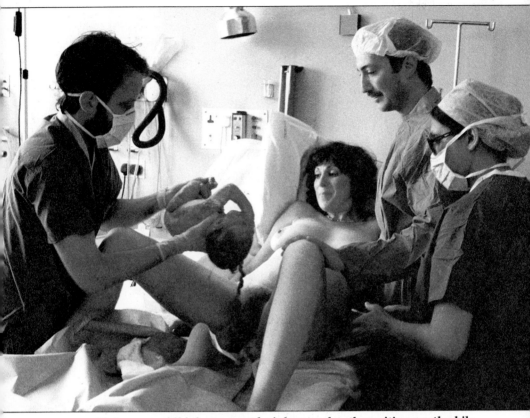

Seeing your child the moment he is born makes the waiting worthwhile.

and ease the passage of the baby's head may also be performed.

Once fathers were asked to leave the delivery room if forceps were used. Now, this is rarely the case.

Forceps may leave red marks on the side of your baby's head. These do not indicate damage and should soon fade.

Don't let your wife feel she has failed to have her child naturally if she has a forceps delivery. Forceps are used for a purpose.

33. *What is a vacuum extraction?*

This procedure is also known as a *ventouse*. A vacuum extraction involves use of a flat suction cup made of metal. It is fitted through a tube to a vacuum pump, and the cup is pushed against the baby's head. Having created a vacuum, the doctor pulls on the tube to deliver the baby.

This method of delivery is sometimes used instead of forceps. It is often done at the start of the second stage of labor. Usually the mother has epidural anesthesia. Because of the suction action, the baby may be born with a slight swelling on his head. This usually disappears within a few hours.

36. *Will the doctor allow me to cut the cord?*

Cutting the cord may add to your sense of participation in the birth. Ask about it in advance. When a father is present at the birth, the doctor may invite him to do so.

37. *I have heard the placenta may be retained. Is this true?*

The placenta is normally expelled a few minutes after the baby is born. An injection of *ergonovine* may even be given to ensure this. Some doctors believe birth of the placenta should be allowed to happen naturally, if possible.

Occasionally, the afterbirth is not expelled. It may have to be removed by the doctor. Anesthesia is given, and the doctor eases out the placenta. This should not affect future pregnancies.

Sometimes a mother may experience heavy loss of bright-red blood. Do not confuse this with the *lochia* that gradually fades in color shortly following the birth. Bright-red blood should be reported to your doctor immediately. It may be an indication some of the placenta was not expelled.

Your wife will probably want to hold the baby immediately after birth.

If you assist at an emergency delivery, keep the placenta so the doctor can check that all the afterbirth was expelled.

38. *I have heard a lot about LeBoyer and his philosophy of birth. How does a LeBoyer birth differ from conventional hospital births?*

Frederick LeBoyer advocates what he calls "birth without violence." Most authorities have concentrated on childbirth from the mother's point of view. They have forgotten what the experience might be like for the baby. LeBoyer's aim is to reduce the trauma of coming into this world—"the torture of the innocent"— as he describes it.

LeBoyer believes the atmosphere in which your

baby is born is important. For 9 months, the baby has lived in darkness and silence in the womb. Any sudden change will shock him.

With a LeBoyer birth, lighting is subdued. Your baby is sensitive to light and may have perceived it in the womb as a golden haze. Harsh glare may frighten him. Your baby can also hear, so any sounds he encounters at birth should be soft. Photographs taken at a LeBoyer birth show the babies calm, but alert.

As soon as the baby is born, he is placed on his mother's abdomen. She can stroke and caress him. He is still attached by the cord. LeBoyer believes it should not be clamped until it has stopped pulsating. To do so before is an "act of cruelty." The baby shouldn't be held upside down and slapped. His first cry should come naturally. Both parents should be given the opportunity to spend time cradling the newborn, so bonding may occur.

LeBoyer advocates placing the baby in a bath of warm water, reminiscent of the fluid of the amniotic sac. Calm and serene, the baby will usually open his eyes and reach out with his hands. The environment of birth, according to LeBoyer, can have a strong impact on the emotional development of your baby, even a lifelong effect.

You may find your hospital has adopted some of these procedures. For instance, a baby is usually placed on the mother's abdomen immediately after birth. However, for most parents, the usual birth environment is the traditional delivery room.

39. *What do I do if we have an emergency delivery?*

Like most potential fathers, you probably dread the thought of having to cope with an emergency delivery. The following guidelines will give you the basics, in case the need arises.

Try to get medical help. If you can't get help, don't panic. Birth is a natural event.

1. Help your wife during contractions.

2. Find something to put the baby in after birth if you don't have a crib. A clean box will do. Line it with a towel or clean blanket.

3. Get something to wrap the baby in.

4. Get a bowl for the afterbirth, scissors (which you should sterilize in boiling water), and string or cord. Cut a few pieces of string, about 10 inches long. Boil these, too.

5. Put clean sheets on the bed, or cover it with a plastic sheet. An extra blanket or covering to keep your wife warm is useful.

6. Keep your wife as relaxed as possible. Remind her to use the breathing techniques learned at prenatal classes. Encourage her to rest between contractions.

You may soon see the first sign of the baby's head. It looks like a wrinkled walnut as it emerges, then disappears again.

Scrub your hands and try to improvise a mask. Tell your wife to pant during contractions, with her mouth open. She shouldn't try to force the baby's head out too quickly.

Once the baby's head emerges, the shoulders and body should follow rapidly. Lift the baby up toward his mother's abdomen. Be gentle. Don't pull at the cord. Ease it over the baby's head if it is wrapped around it.

Your baby may have cried soon after birth. If not, hold him head down, but don't smack him on the back. If he still doesn't cry, mouth-to-mouth respiration may be necessary. Repeat it for several minutes.

With a clean piece of gauze, remove any mucus

from his mouth and nose. Lay him on his mother's stomach.

Soon the placenta will be expelled. It looks like a large piece of liver. This has nourished your baby during pregnancy and is usually expelled easily. Don't be worried if there is bleeding at this stage. If it is fairly heavy, rub your wife's abdomen. It should help reduce it. Keep the afterbirth, so the doctor can see if it is complete.

Next, deal with the umbilical cord. First, tie one length of sterilized string 6 inches from the baby's stomach. Tie another piece 6 inches farther down. Wait until the cord stops pulsating, then cut it with the scissors. If there is any sign of blood from the baby's end, tie another piece of string closer to his stomach.

Make your wife as comfortable as possible. She may like a change of clothes. She will need a sanitary napkin.

The kettles of water were for sterilizing the string. They can also be used by your wife to wash and freshen up.

AFTER THE BIRTH

40. *What will happen immediately after the birth?*

Your baby will probably be placed on his mother's abdomen. Mucus will be sucked out of his respiratory tract and any breathing assistance will be given. Your wife will also have any stitches required following the birth.

While this is being done, you may be allowed to hold the baby. He will be wiped clean and your wife will be made comfortable. The baby will have his identification bracelet put on. The child and mother will have the same identification numbers.

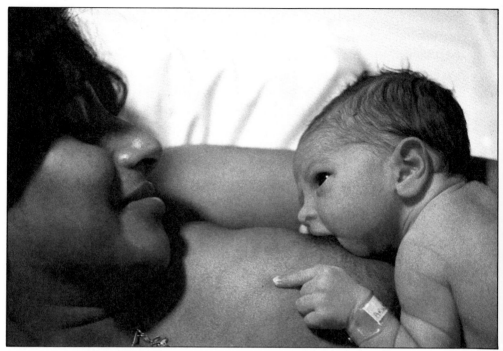

A baby may begin to suck immediately after birth when put to his mother's breast.

By law, drops of silver nitrate or antibiotics will be put into the baby's eyes. This is done to protect him from the effects of gonorrhea. Women can have the disease without being aware of it.

Your wife may be given the baby to nurse immediately, depending on how she feels. You have both just experienced one of the greatest joys of life, so you'll probably want time alone together.

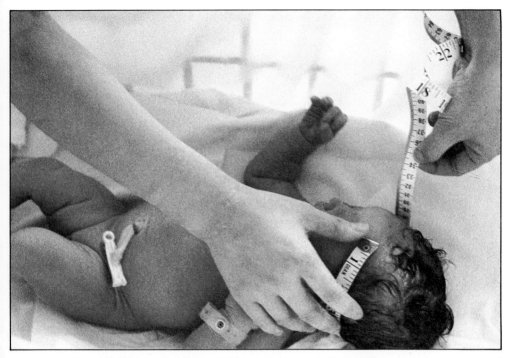

Soon after birth, the doctor will examine your baby. Head circumference is measured, length recorded and hips tested for sign of dislocation.

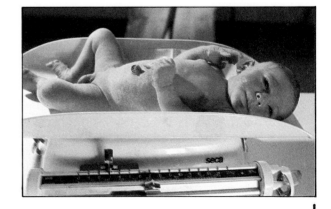

Your baby will also be weighed. The average weight of the newborn is between 6 and 8 pounds.

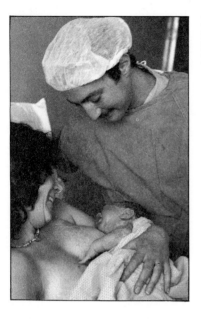

It's wonderful when the waiting is over and you're finally a family. The bonding period is important to get to know your baby.

It's an incredible feeling to hold your new baby for the first time.

41. *Is the bonding period between parents and child after birth important?*

Research indicates it is. Attachment can take place later, so don't worry too much if your baby has to be separated from you both immediately after birth. But even then, you will *both* probably be encouraged to spend as much time as possible with him. Bonding to the father should not be forgotten.

Many doctors like to place the baby on his mother's abdomen for early bonding to take place. Skin contact is important. You will probably be allowed time together with the baby after the birth. You can become acquainted with him in a loving way. Caress him, stroke his face, arms and legs.

42. *Why are some babies taken away from their mothers soon after birth? Isn't rooming-in more favorable?*

When the baby is allowed to remain in a crib beside his mother's bed for most or all of the time, it

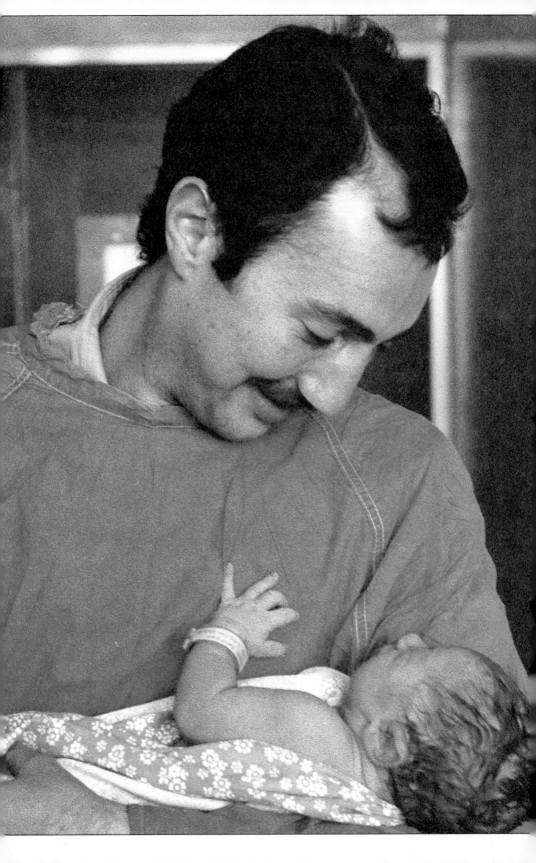

is called *rooming-in*. This helps a mother adjust to her baby. Rooming-in is not the practice in all hospitals. Babies are usually taken to a nursery after a Caesarean section or if the mother is unwell. The baby will go to the nursery when it is premature or ill.

If your wife has the choice, she may decide to have the baby with her. She will be able to establish feeding more easily, care for him and hold him when she wants to.

43. *Why is an injection sometimes given to a mother after the birth of her baby?*

The bloodstream of mother and baby do not usually mix. But a small amount of the baby's blood may cross to the mother during pregnancy or delivery. This may happen to the Rh-negative mother of an Rh-positive baby. The mother's body will begin to produce antibodies to destroy the invading cells.

The mother won't be sensitized against Rh-positive cells. Her body will produce antibodies if she has another Rh-positive baby. The antibodies could then cross the placenta to the baby and destroy his red-blood cells. This could cause anemia and other serious Rh problems.

An injection of RHO-GAM is given to an Rh-negative mother within three days after the birth. This keeps antibodies from forming that may be harmful to future babies.

44. *The doctor has indicated our baby may be small at birth. Will he be put in an incubator? Will Alice be able to feed him?*

Often babies are put in incubators after birth, no matter what size or weight they are. They spend the first six hours in the "temperature-maintained

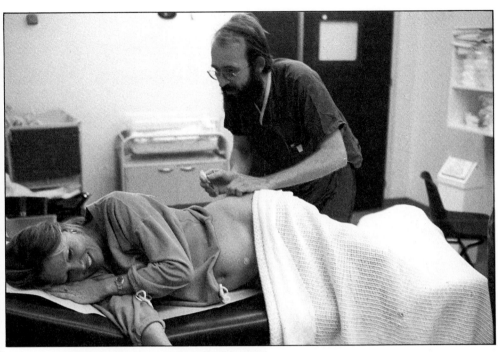

The Rh-negative mother who has an Rh-positive baby is given an injection of RHO-GAM within 72 hours of the birth. This keeps problems from occurring in subsequent pregnancies.

environment" of an incubator. This helps stabilize their body temperature.

Many premature babies spend some time in an incubator. If a baby is premature and swallowing and sucking reflexes are developed, tube feeding may not be necessary. You both may be able to feed him, perhaps even with breast milk if your wife expresses her milk.

A larger premature baby may be able to feed from the breast. You will probably be encouraged to feed him yourselves. Research shows early parental bonding is important to the development of a healthy parent-child relationship.

If a baby has difficulty breathing or is very small, he may have to be transferred to a neonatal intensive-care unit. He will not be separated from his mother unless absolutely necessary. This is a rare occurrence.

45. *How long will Harriet have to stay in bed after the birth?*

The nurses will encourage her to get up a few hours after the birth. This improves circulation of blood in the lower part of the body and minimizes risk of blood clots.

46. *How long will Jean be in the hospital after the birth of our first child?*

The length of stay varies. It will depend on the progress of both mother and baby following the birth. There is a trend toward 48-hour stays, if the mother feels good. If your wife feels she needs to stay a little longer, ask your doctor about it.

47. *What will the hospital routine be like for Sandy?*

The new mother needs a lot of rest the first few days after the birth. Hospital routine can be tiring, and your wife may have little time to herself. You might restrict visiting to close family and friends.

During the day, she will be busy feeding the baby, changing diapers, holding him and seeing the doctor. Her night may be disturbed by the 2 a.m. feeding.

Many women feel uncomfortable after the birth, especially if they had stitches. Bowel movements may be a problem, especially after stitches. The nurses will check on this.

48. *Will Maggie suffer pains or cramps after the birth?*

It's not unusual for a mother to complain of mild pains in her abdomen for a few days after the birth. Stimulation of the breasts during feeding causes contractions of the uterus, helping it return to its normal size.

A mild analgesic may be prescribed by the doctor. Your wife should not take any drugs without talking to her doctor. Drugs can affect her breast milk. A mother who has had a Caesarean will feel uncomfortable until the scar heals. Pain may also be felt after an episiotomy.

49. *Why did Angela feel cold immediately after the birth of our child?*

Some women experience shivering toward the end of the first stage of labor. They need a blanket or a hot water bottle. Socks may also be appreciated. When shivering occurs later, it may be due to loss of heat or to an emotional reaction after the birth is over.

50. *I've heard the term "transfiguration" used to describe a woman following the birth of her child. What does it mean?*

It's a special phenomenon. You may notice it if you're with your wife at the birth. Look at her when it's all over and she is holding your baby. She glows with pride, relief and joy at the miracle of the newborn. This reaction and the change in the mother immediately following the birth is called the *transfiguration.*

VISITING AT THE HOSPITAL

51. Do you recommend we take our 4-year-old to the hospital to see the new baby?

Your wife may leave the hospital soon after the birth of your child. It's probably a good idea to take your son with you, if the hospital allows it. He may not understand where mommy has gone. He may not realize the new baby has arrived.

Let him see the baby, and introduce him as the big brother. Give your wife time to be affectionate toward him. She should reassure him he is not forgotten. Let him help take care of the baby. It may help him with his feelings of jealousy.

52. Should Janet have visitors immediately after the birth?

It may be hard to stop relatives and friends from coming to the hospital. Your wife will need rest for the first few days after the birth. Her body needs time to readjust after the pregnancy.

Ask her who she would like to see while she is in the hospital. If she gets tired while they are there, she can let them know.

53. What will we have to do to register the birth of our baby?

The hospital will advise you of the appropriate procedure. In the hospital, your wife may fill out some forms naming your child. In some places, you have a certain amount of time to name the baby.

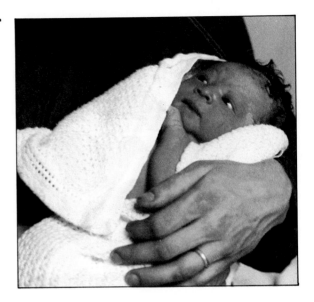

It may be difficult to keep friends and relatives from coming to the hospital to see your new baby.

OTHER QUESTIONS ABOUT BIRTH

54. *What is a birthing center?*

This is a new idea and still experimental, so your hospital may not have one. A birthing center provides an environment like a home. Delivery rooms look like bedrooms. Up-to-date equipment is still close at hand if it is needed.

The baby is able to remain with his mother after the birth, not taken to another room. Expert attention and all the equipment needed in case of an emergency are available. The warm, homelike atmosphere helps put the mother at ease.

55. *What is natural childbirth?*

This method of childbirth keeps the experience as joyful as possible. It may be called *natural childbirth*, but a mother has to prepare for it. She must learn various techniques to help with the process. Natural childbirth doesn't promise pain-free labor. It's a total approach, designed to give knowledge and confidence.

In natural childbirth, the mother goes into labor spontaneously. Little pain relief is given so she can be aware of what is going on throughout the birth. She is able to concentrate on specific breathing and relaxation techniques.

As the father, you will have an important part to play in natural childbirth. You will practice "natural" methods of pain relief with your wife.

Your wife may feel strongly about not taking drugs during labor. She may want to have the baby as naturally as possible. Tell the doctor this is what she prefers. However, she should not be upset if the doctor must intervene for some reason. Ask him to explain why he is doing so.

56. *We just had a false alarm. Patty thought labor had started yesterday, but the doctor sent her home. Why did this happen?*

Your wife may have felt contractions that occur throughout pregnancy, called *Braxton-Hicks contractions*. These contractions are usually painless, although they may cause some discomfort at night.

Labor contractions are not the same. Your wife will notice the difference when they start. They are more regular, become stronger and the interval between them gradually decreases. The discomfort your wife felt may have been from constipation or pressure on the bowel from your baby.

There is no reason for a woman to feel embarrassed about a false alarm. It's common. Even the doctor and experienced labor-room nurses can't always tell whether true labor has started without a period of observation. The woman, her husband and the doctor should take these false alarms with good humor.

57. What is the afterbirth?

The afterbirth is also known as the *placenta*. It was the link between your baby and his mother in the womb. It provided the baby with food and oxygen. It can even excrete waste products. A placenta may have other functions, including production of hormones that help prevent ovulation and menstruation during pregnancy. It also prepares the body for breast-feeding.

A placenta weighs about a pound and is dark red and spongelike. It is expelled a few minutes after the birth of your baby, in the third stage of labor. An injection may be given to the woman as the baby is born. This causes the uterus to contract so the placenta will be delivered quickly.

The doctor carefully examines the placenta to make sure it is complete. If part of it remains, it can cause severe bleeding days after delivery. It is then necessary to remove it from the uterus under anesthesia.

Identical twins share the same placenta. Fraternal twins develop from two separately fertilized eggs. They each have their own placenta.

If the placenta blocks the neck of the womb and the baby's passage through the birth canal, it is called *placenta previa*. A Caesarean section is often necessary with this condition.

58. *The doctor told Martha she will probably have a Caesarean section. What does this involve? Are there aftereffects?*

A Caesarean section involves surgically removing a baby from the womb. There are several reasons why it may be done. There may be risk to the life of mother, baby or both. The mother's pelvis may be too small for the baby's head. The mother may be diabetic and have a large baby. There may be risk of labor being prolonged. Induction may have failed for some reason, or there may be signs of fetal distress. There may be a transverse presentation, with the baby lying across the uterus. Placenta previa, with the afterbirth lying across the neck of the womb, may be a complication.

In some hospitals, doctors do a Caesarean if the mother is over 35 and there are any problems. Once doctors may have tried to turn a breech baby. Many now prefer to do a Caesarean section.

There are many cases where a Caesarean may be advisable. It has been estimated that as many as 20% of all births are now Caesarean sections.

Your wife may be given a general anesthetic. You will probably not be permitted to remain with her if this happens. She may have the Caesarean under epidural anesthesia. This means she will be fully conscious and you may be able to stay.

An I.V. will be set up in case additional fluid is required or a transfusion is needed. To perform a Caesarean section, an incision is usually made in the lower part of the abdominal wall. It is made horizontally, along the bikini line, so the resulting scar is not obvious.

The operation takes about 45 minutes. Internal stitches usually dissolve within a few days. External ones are removed in about a week.

Some doctors believe once a Caesarean section is

done, the mother must always have a Caesarean. Others believe a normal delivery in a subsequent pregnancy may be possible.

For a while, your wife's abdomen will be tender. But she will be given pain-relieving drugs to help with this. In about two days, she will be able to get up and walk around. This avoids risk of blood clots in her legs. It may take time before she feels well, and she may need help at home. It will be a few weeks before she feels good enough to start postnatal exercises.

It may seem there are disadvantages to a Caesarean, but there is a plus. Most people say Caesarean babies are more beautiful when born. They have not suffered the molding of the head that often occurs during the normal vaginal journey.

59. *Some friends' baby was delivered by a nurse midwife. What is a nurse midwife?*

New on the North American obstetrical scene is the nurse midwife. She is a birth attendant who helps a mother with the normal delivery of her baby. A nurse midwife may provide the woman with prenatal care and attends her during labor and delivery.

Often a nurse midwife is associated with a doctor. She sees the pregnant woman at the doctor's office and works with her in prenatal care. She also helps the woman prepare for natural childbirth, teaching her exercises and breathing techniques. When it is time for the baby to be born, the nurse midwife meets the woman at the hospital. She stays with her until the baby is born.

A nurse midwife attends a normal delivery and is alert for any problems. If a problem occurs, a doctor is called in to deliver the baby.

60. *What kind of training does a midwife have?*

There are two types of midwives—the nurse midwife and the empirical midwife. The *nurse midwife* is a registered nurse who continues training to become a midwife. She participates in a program of study lasting from one to two years. The program is offered by an accredited school of midwifery. The nurse is awarded a certificate from the school, then she must pass an examination. In the U.S., when she fulfills these requirements, she is licensed by the state. In Canada, midwifery is just gaining acceptance. Contact your province health office for more information. Most nurse midwives work with doctors or at clinics, delivering babies at hospitals.

An *empirical midwife* has no formal training. She serves a type of apprenticeship and usually delivers babies at home. An empirical midwife may or may not be licensed, depending on where she practices.

61. *What can a nurse midwife do?*

A nurse midwife attends a normal delivery of a baby who is born by natural childbirth. The philosophy of midwives is if a woman needs pain relief, it is an option that will not be denied. But a delivery attended by a midwife does not use pain relief as a matter of course.

A nurse midwife can perform an episiotomy if it is needed. Some clinics in large cities use nurse midwives at all normal births. This allows the doctors to concentrate on problem births.

62. *Our baby was born early and is in an incubator. What are the functions of an incubator? How long will our baby have to stay in the hospital?*

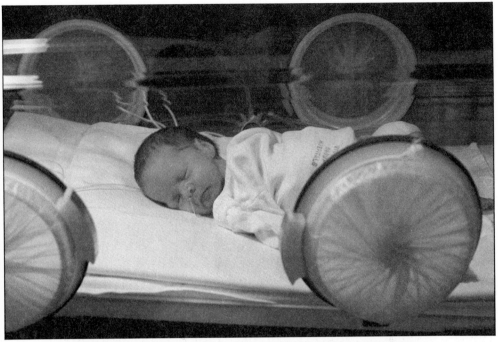

If your baby is premature, he may be put in an incubator. You'll be encouraged to spend as much time with him as possible. When he catches up in size, breathes normally and takes nourishment, he'll be allowed to go home. In a short time, no one will know he wasn't a full-term baby.

An incubator creates an environment similar to the womb. Your baby's system may not be sufficiently developed to cope without help. An incubator helps the baby by controlling temperature, humidity and oxygen intake. It will protect your baby from sources of infection.

Most incubators have a see-through top and sides so you can see your baby. Portholes permit access. If your baby must stay in an incubator, you will be encouraged to be with him as much as possible.

Your wife may be able to go home, but it may be some time before the baby can join you. Your doctor will advise you about this. You will both probably be able to visit as often as you wish.

63. *Is it true some women find giving birth sexually stimulating?*

Some women say they found it so, particularly during the second stage of labor. This is the stage during which the baby is actually born. It's hard work, but it is an exciting and emotional moment for the mother. Some mothers have described the feeling as "orgasmic."

64. *Can you tell me something about birth in water?*

This was pioneered in the Soviet Union and is designed to recreate the environment of the womb. The experience of birth in water is supposed to be less of a shock to the baby. The water is heated to body temperature and the mother is submerged in it. This is supposed to relax the mother and result in less discomfort for her. Theoretically, the baby comes into the world more readily, with greater ease. This method has not been experimented with greatly in North America.

Living with Baby

Sometimes it's love at first sight when you meet your baby. Sometimes it takes longer for a bond to be established. Adapting to parenthood takes time, effort and understanding. Suddenly you are responsible for this new life. You may be anxious about caring for him.

Start with an equal partnership. You'll find looking after your developing infant is easier and more enjoyable if you and your wife share the work. Your role as the participating father is a valuable one.

ABOUT YOUR BABY

1. *It is only three days since our baby was born. We're worried because he has lost weight.*

There's no need to worry. Weight loss is normal during the first few days of life. The few lost ounces will usually be regained by the end of the first or second week.

Babies are born with some extra fluid in their bodies. Fluid is excreted from the kidneys, bladder, bowel and through perspiration.

It takes a few days for your baby to feed well enough to obtain sufficient calories for growth. His food stores allow for this. If weight loss persists or your baby is not back to his birth weight at the two-week checkup, your doctor will advise you what to do.

2. *Is it true a baby is born with certain reflexes?*

A baby is born with many reflexes, so watch for them after birth. One that is soon lost is the *walking reflex*. Your pediatrician may test for it. He holds the

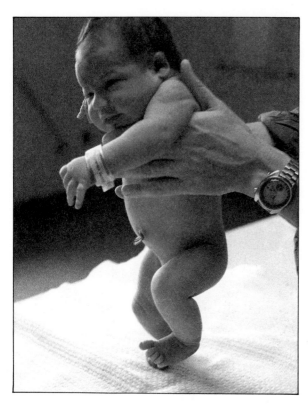

A newborn baby is born with several reflexes, but loses some soon after birth. His walking reflex is pronounced. If he is held under his arms, he will lift one leg as if trying to move forward. Other reflexes with which he is born include sucking, grasping, rooting and swallowing.

baby so his feet touch the ground, and a stepping movement ensues.

Try putting your finger in the palm of your newborn baby's hand. His fingers grasp it. His toes will curl around your finger if you touch the sole of his foot. This is the *grasp reflex*. Startle him, and he'll arch his body, throw out his arms and spread his hands wide. This is called the *Moro reflex*. Other reflexes such as *rooting, sucking* and *swallowing* are developed at birth.

3. *I've heard a newborn's head is sensitive. Is this true?*

At birth your baby's development is not complete. At the top of his head is a soft spot, called the *fontanelle.* The fontanelle is covered by a tough

Your newborn may look delicate, but babies are hardy. When you pick him up, be sure to protect his head.

membrane. Beneath the membrane, the bones of the skull are not joined. This is normal. Be careful with his head, but don't worry about it. A newborn baby is not as fragile as he looks.

4. Why is our newborn's skin mottled?

This is a common skin appearance in a baby. You may notice it after a bath. It may be attributed to the baby's developing circulatory system. It will soon disappear.

Don't worry if the baby's hands and feet seem a little blue at first. This is called *acrocyarosis* and is normal, as long as the rest of the body is pink.

5. I'm perturbed about our baby's appearance.

The doctor will tell you if there is anything wrong. Few newborn babies are beautiful when they're born. Don't be surprised if your baby is not pretty.

The face may be puffy, and the head may seem lopsided. It will soon change shape. The buttocks may look skinny because muscles are not fully developed. Perhaps the stump left by the cord looks odd. It will soon dry up and drop off. The red marks on the eyelids or nape of the neck will fade, too.

Don't worry about these things. Even a raised "strawberry mark," due to a proliferation of blood vessels on the surface, disappears in time.

6. Why is our newborn's head so floppy? Is something wrong?

It will be two to three months before your baby will be able to support his head. Now, his muscles are not developed enough to hold it up. This is normal. Be sure to support his head and shoulders when you pick him up.

7. Why does our baby have cradle cap?

Cradle cap is common in early infancy and is a form of *seborrheic dermatitis.* The scalp gets scaly patches, sometimes with a yellow crust. This condition is not serious, but don't ignore it. If it persists, consult your doctor. Careful washing with a special shampoo helps remove the scales. Soften them with baby oil before you bathe him.

8. Our baby has some blue-gray marks on his back. Should we worry about them?

These marks, sometimes called *mongolian spots,* are not connected with Down's syndrome. Spots are

Your baby's muscles are not yet strong enough to hold his head. You need to support and protect it when you lift or carry him.

common in dark-skinned babies. They usually fade or disappear in a few months. They are due to an excess of pigment in the skin.

9. *Our baby has fine hairs on parts of his body. Is this normal?*

These fine body hairs are called *lanugo,* from the Latin word for wool. They are often present when a baby is born early. Your baby's body was covered with hair while he was in the womb. Most of it was shed before birth.

He may also have a lot of hair on his head when he is born. This may also be partly lost.

10. *Our baby's eyes don't seem to focus correctly. What should we do about this?*

Most newborn babies squint a little. Their eye muscles are not strong. The wandering of the eyes should disappear by the time he is 6 months old. If not, consult your doctor.

11. *Our week-old baby has dark-blue eyes, but I've heard the color may change. Is this true?*

Almost all newborn babies have blue or gray eyes. If they remain that color after four weeks or so, they will probably stay that shade. But you can't be sure about eye color until your baby is 8 or 9 months old.

12. *How long will it be before our baby's navel heals?*

It takes one to three weeks for the stump of the umbilical cord to wither and drop off. Keep the area around it clean and dry. Your doctor will advise you about cleaning it with alcohol. You may also be advised to leave it uncovered. It may leave a raw spot, but this soon heals. Redness of the skin around the cord, pus or foul odor from the cord are signs of infection. If these occur, consult your doctor.

13. *There are small white spots on our newborn baby's face. What are they?*

The small white spots are called *milia*. They often appear on a baby's face a few weeks after birth, but are sometimes present at birth. They are blocked oil glands in the skin. Ignore them and they will soon disappear.

The amount of hair a baby has at birth varies. Your child may have a full head of hair, then lose it. It will be replaced by new hair, maybe of a different color.

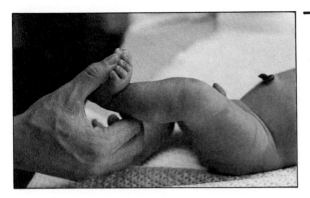

The stump of the umbilical cord drops off after about a week. The scar which remains is the navel. Don't be concerned if it protrudes. This is normal and it soon takes on the more common appearance.

14. *Can our newborn baby see? He seems aware of what's going on around him.*

It used to be thought the newborn couldn't see at all, that babies were born blind. We now know differently. A newborn baby is sensitive to movement and light. Watch his pupils adjust according to the amount of light in the room. A newborn will also briefly follow faces or bright objects.

He can see some color from an early age. However, he has not yet developed full vision.

15. *Can a newborn hear?*

Yes, your baby can hear. There is even evidence that the baby can hear inside the womb. Some babies respond to noise from the environment outside the mother. A newborn will startle or turn briefly to auditory stimuli, such as a bell or rattle.

Babies can see from birth, although their vision remains limited for a few weeks.

16. *Our baby girl had a vaginal discharge of mucus and blood at birth, almost like a menstrual period. Could anything be wrong?*

You may have noticed her diaper was stained with blood. All female babies have a mucoid vaginal discharge. Sometimes this is also accompanied by a small amount of vaginal bleeding. This is normal and results from the effect of the maternal hormones on the baby. These symptoms will usually disappear in the first week or so.

17. *Would you recommend circumcision for our baby boy?*

Circumcision is the removal of the foreskin that covers the tip of the penis. Jewish and Moslem religions require circumcision be done soon after birth. In some places, circumcision is a standard procedure, while in others, it is not.

Circumcision is believed by many to be hygenic. The secretions of the penis don't collect underneath the foreskin and cause infection. But there is no definite evidence to support this.

Discuss it with your pediatrician. It is a matter of personal choice. However, circumcision is usually done soon after birth, if it's going to be done.

18. *Are night feedings necessary?*

A newborn baby usually needs to be fed every four hours, sometimes more often at first. Night feedings are essential. This means your sleep has to be disturbed for a while.

If the last feeding is 11:00 p.m., your baby may sleep through until 4:00 a.m. This won't be usual until he is about 2 months old. After that, it's a matter of timing and personal choice. You may decide to go to bed early and get up for an early feeding, or go to bed later and get up later.

If you are demand feeding, you will feed him whenever your baby requires it. But don't jump at his slightest whimper. He may just have awakened for a second and will go back to sleep again.

19. *Our baby cries a lot. Could something be wrong?*

All babies cry—it's the only way they can attract attention. Continual crying can be distressing for new parents. You want to rush to his side, yet you don't know what to do. You aren't sure of the reason for his crying.

In the first few weeks, hunger is usually the primary cause. A feeding will comfort him. Your baby may also be crying because he needs to suck. A pacifier may help, but don't give him one when he's hungry.

Crying may be a sign of discomfort. He may be too warm or too cold, or the diaper may be wet or soiled. He may have indigestion, gas or colic. A baby may cry out of a desire for bodily contact and affection.

One of the best ways to soothe him, when it's not hunger or discomfort, is to pick him up and rock him. Talk to him and distract his attention. Walk around with him while you continue what you are doing. Being close to you should calm him. Soon you will be able to interpret his different cries.

20. *Our baby cries a lot, but we never see any tears. Is this normal?*

All small babies cry, but it's rare to see tears until the baby is a couple of months old. Before then, the tear ducts carry away any tear solution produced.

21. *What changes can I expect to see in our baby in the next year?*

It's exciting to watch your baby grow, but there is no exact timetable for his development. All babies sit, feed themselves, crawl and walk at their own rate. However, there are certain age ranges for milestones to normally occur. Your doctor will notice if there are any developmental delays.

Within a few weeks, you will learn to recognize your baby's different cries. You will know whether he's hungry, distressed, lonely or bored.

Measure a premature baby's development from the expected date of delivery, not the actual birth date. HPBooks' *Your Baby's First 30 Months* and *Child Care From Birth To Age 5* can help you have a better understanding of the physical and social developments of your baby.

During his first month, your baby will start to watch your face intently. He may be startled by sudden noises, but grows quiet when you pick him up. By 6 weeks old, he may respond with a smile. He cries, but there are no real tears. He can usually be comforted by a soft voice. He sleeps from feeding to feeding.

During his second month, there is progress. Soon he is able to hold his head up for a few seconds. When held in a sitting position, he turns his head. He grows quiet when he hears a noise. He moves his arms and legs when lying on his back. He sheds tears when he cries and makes cooing noises. He responds to bright colors. Playing with him in the bath is fun, because he is learning how to splash.

Chatting to your baby at this stage is important. He won't understand what you say, but he can understand your tone.

22. How aware will our baby be by 12 weeks?

Although he is probably sleeping between 16 and 18 hours a day, your baby will be responsive to you by this time. Keep a log of his development, and make daily or weekly notes about progress. It's fascinating to watch a baby grow, but babies develop at their own rate. These are only *general* guidelines.

A baby can usually hold up his head by 3 months old. He may also lift his chest when lying on his tummy. He'll probably stare at a mobile hung over his crib. He will kick in the water when you bathe him, and he puts everything in his mouth. He's strong when he grasps your finger, too. He may have dropped one night feeding so your sleep is less disturbed.

23. Our newborn baby sneezes a lot. Does she have a cold?

It's common for small babies to sneeze. Your baby doesn't have a cold. It's just an efficient means of clearing nasal passages.

24. Our baby was born prematurely and is in the neonatal care unit. How often will we be able to see him? How long will it be before we can bring him home?

It may upset you to see your baby in an incubator. He looks small and frail, with so many tubes attached to him. But he is in the best environment for him until he is stronger.

He may be delicate, but he is probably active. He will open his eyes, respond to sound, light and touch, and will cry. His arms and legs look skinny and wrinkled. His head may seem large and out of proportion with the rest of his body. His breathing and heartbeat may be monitored constantly. He may also have jaundice.

The incubator is a type of cradle with a transparent cover. It maintains correct temperature for your baby. Special portholes at the side allow you to touch your baby. It's important for both of you to spend as much time as possible with him. This will help the parental bond develop.

Your baby may be fed through a tube in his nose. Nutrients may be fed into a vein if he can't tolerate formula. Your wife may even be able to express breast milk so he can be fed her milk.

In some instances, a baby remains in special care after his mother has left the hospital. You will be encouraged to be involved in his daily care.

Doing something for your baby will help you feel confident about your ability to care for him. Visiting may not be restricted. Studies show when there is early separation and lack of contact, parents may not readily accept the child as their own.

Doctors don't recommend a definite size or weight when a premature baby may safely go home. They usually wait until the baby is feeding well from the breast or bottle, and can be treated like a full-term baby.

You won't feel relaxed about his well-being until he is safely home with you. But don't worry about his development. Some people say a normal premature baby may be more intelligent than a full-term baby.

BOTTLE-FEEDING BABY

25. Is it possible to breast- and bottle-feed?

You may be tempted to give a bottle of formula if the baby is fussy or still hungry. Avoid this. Your wife's breasts need to be stimulated by the feeding baby to give sufficient milk. A bottle will interrupt the demand-and-supply sequence. Offer a bottle only if the baby is distressed or your wife is absent and she hasn't expressed her own milk. Don't make it a routine procedure.

26. *What is colostrum?*

About the third day after the birth, your wife's breast milk will come in. Prior to this, the breasts secrete a substance that is thicker and creamier than milk, called *colostrum.*

Colostrum is yellow and rich in proteins. It acts as a lining for your baby's stomach. It protects him from bacteria when he might be susceptible to infection. It also provides him with certain antibodies against diseases to which his mother is resistant.

There is no artificial equivalent to colostrum. Colostrum is easy to digest because of its low-fat content. It is an excellent starter food. It also has a mild laxative effect. It will help the baby get rid of stools accumulated while in the womb.

Mothers are advised to nurse frequently the first few days. This helps milk production. Also the newborn can receive the full benefit of the available colostrum.

27. *Jane is planning to return to work soon. Would it be best for her to breast-feed for a few weeks, then bottle-feed, or bottle-feed from birth?*

This is a question commonly asked by women intending to go back to work. Try to combine the two. Your wife can breast-feed the baby when she's home. While at work, your baby can be bottle-fed by the person who is looking after him. Your wife may be able to express sufficient milk for one bottle, if she works part-time.

Your wife may plan to bottle-feed only after she returns to work. If she does, she should breast-feed, even if for a limited time. Then your baby will have the benefits of breast milk during his first few weeks or months. It's better for him to have some breast milk than none at all. Breast milk, like colostrum, contains substances that help prevent infection in the baby.

28. *Lucy has decided against breast-feeding. Will she be given something to dry up her milk?*

Special hormones may be given to a mother who has chosen not to breast-feed. This keeps the milk from coming to her breasts. It's actually the baby's sucking that stimulates the milk supply. If your wife is not breast-feeding, the milk flow will not be encouraged.

29. *Andrea has decided she would prefer to bottle-feed. Will our baby be deprived?*

Many doctors feel breast-feeding is best for babies. But if a woman isn't happy about it, she should bottle-feed. She should not feel guilty about her decision. What is best for her is probably best for the baby, too.

What is imporant is *how* your baby is fed. You and your wife will both be able to feed the baby. Hold the baby close when feeding. This kind of contact is necessary for bonding.

As children grow up, it's impossible to distinguish between breast- and bottle-fed babies. Your infant will not be deprived.

Breast-feeding may be best for your newborn baby. If your wife can't breast-feed or doesn't want to, the baby will not be deprived.

30. What is formula?

Formula is a milk product for feeding a baby. It is made from cow's milk and water, with added sugar, minerals, vitamins and other nutrients.

Formula may come in cans, packages or bottles. Some formula is dry and must be mixed with water before use. Some formula is ready-to-feed. There is also a liquid concentrate that needs water added to it. There are special types of formula, such as soy formula, for babies who can't tolerate the usual formulas.

Most babies thrive on formula. It is modified to be more suitable than ordinary cow's milk. Ordinary cow's milk is not easily digested by an infant and also contains little iron. If a baby drinks only cow's milk, it can result in iron-deficiency anemia.

If you bottle-feed your baby, you and your wife can share this task together. It will help in the bonding process.

Talk to your pediatrician about sterilizing bottles and nipples. What you have to sterilize, and for how long, depends on where you live and the water supply you use.

31. *How much and how often should we bottle-feed our baby?*

Allow about 3 ounces of formula, plus your baby's age in months, per feeding until 5 to 6 months old. Then he will take an 8-ounce bottle. A 2-month-old would take 5 ounces: $3 + 2 = 5$ ounces.

If you are feeding on demand, your baby will probably need a bottle about every three to four hours. You can make a quart of formula at a time.

Follow formula instructions carefully. If you have any questions, consult your doctor.

32. Should our baby's formula be warm?

It may be more comforting for a baby to have warm milk, but it is not necessary. If your baby seems anxious for a feeding, you could give a cold bottle. Always keep formula that is made up in the refrigerator. It's safe to keep a 24-hour supply. If you're going out, take cold formula with you. You can heat it in a bottle warmer.

33. What sort of bottle is best for our baby?

A drugstore will have a large selection of bottles. Plastic ones are lightweight and unbreakable. If you are traveling, it may be useful to have one with a nipple that can be inverted. Plastic bottles, with presterilized, disposable liners, are also handy. Experiment with the size and type of nipple you need.

You will probably need about six bottles. Keep them covered when not in use.

34. Will our bottle-fed baby put on too much weight?

With breast-feeding, milk supply is linked to demand. With bottle-feeding, it's easy to feed too much formula. Encouraging your baby to eat more than he needs may cause bad habits.

Your baby should gain about 4 to 7 ounces each week. If he is gaining more, you may be feeding him when he is thirsty. Try offering him water at the end of a feeding, instead of more milk. See if he is satisfied. Never add sugar to his bottle. This will cause him to gain weight unnecessarily.

35. *Our baby is being bottle-fed. I'd like to feed him sometimes. Are there any things I should keep in mind? Will being fed by both of us disturb our baby?*

Being fed by strangers might unsettle a baby. But he shouldn't have any trouble getting accustomed to both of you. You'll probably enjoy it, too.

Discuss with your doctor the kind of formula to give your baby. Follow the manufacturer's instructions for making formula. Allow about 3 ounces of formula, plus your baby's age in months per feeding, until 5 to 6 months old. Then he will take an 8-ounce bottle. A 2-month-old would take 5 ounces: $3 + 2 = 5$ ounces. He will need five to six feedings every 24 hours at first. Make the formula, using boiled water that has cooled.

Discuss hygiene with your doctor. He will advise you about sterilizing water, bottles, nipples and utensils. Sterilizing depends on the water you use.

To feed your baby, hold him in your arms. Keep his head raised. Don't let him lie flat when feeding him, and don't leave him alone. Keep the bottle tilted as you feed him, so the milk flow is not interrupted. Be sure the nipple isn't blocked.

36. *I understand there are special formulas available for infants who are allergic to milk.*

Some babies can't tolerate regular formulas and are allergic to them. Formula made from special mixtures, such as soybeans, are available. These can be given in a bottle in the normal way. Your doctor

Some babies may be weaned by 3 months. Others are content with breast milk until 6 months old or older.

will advise you about the type of formula that is best for your baby.

BREAST-FEEDING BABY

37. What are the principal advantages of breast-feeding?

Breast-feeding is best for a baby if his mother is happy about it. Understanding the benefits of breast-feeding may encourage your wife to try it. You should both consider the following points:

- Breast milk is the perfect food for your baby. It's the right temperature, doesn't cost anything and probably won't make your baby fat.
- Breast-feeding will help your wife get her figure back more quickly. It will help her internal organs return to normal.
- The colostrum and milk produced by the breasts gives baby a higher resistance to infection.

- A breast-fed baby's diapers are more pleasant to change. Stools are less foul smelling.
- Breast-feeding is more efficient when traveling. Your baby's food is always ready and there are no bottles to make.
- Breast-fed babies don't usually have digestive troubles.
- A breast-fed baby has close physical contact with his mother.
- There is little risk of milk allergy.

38. *Are there disadvantages to breast-feeding?*

Breast-feeding can be rewarding for a mother and beneficial to her baby. But there are disadvantages, too. A breast-fed baby may need more-frequent nursing. The supply of milk may be affected by the mother's state of health. A mother who breast-feeds is more tied to her baby.

39. *Sally would like to breast-feed our baby. Is there anything I can do to help her with this?*

Spend time with your wife when she starts to breast-feed. It may give her more confidence. Studies show women whose husbands do not want them to breast-feed rarely succeed at it. Your attitude is influential.

40. *How long should Karen feed, and how often?*

There is no easy answer to this question. At first, she might feed seven minutes on each breast, gradually increasing the time to 10 minutes. She should alternate the breast she starts with. The baby usually takes the most milk in the first few minutes.

Some babies want to suck at the breast about every three hours at first, some more regularly. Frequent nursing helps establish the milk more quickly.

41. *Will Helena be able to breast-feed our twins?*

Breast-feeding is a matter of supply equaling demand. It should be possible for your wife to breast-feed twins. It's even possible to feed both simultaneously, but you'll probably find one will wait. You can comfort him with a pacifier until it's his turn.

Your twins may be small at birth and need a lot of care. Your wife will also need a lot of rest following the birth. Twins will be twice the work, but they are also twice the delight.

42. *Is breast-feeding painful?*

Sometimes breast-feeding can be a little painful. Any discomfort won't be too bad and doesn't last long. Pain is usually due to the baby's gums grasping only the nipple, instead of the areola. Special creams are available to help ease soreness and discomfort.

43. *Does Carmen need to eat more while breast-feeding?*

A healthy, well-balanced diet is important while your wife is feeding, for her sake and the baby's. Most doctors recommend an additional intake of 500 to 600 calories a day. In actual foods, this should come from fresh meat, fish, fruit and vegetables. Your wife should also drink as much water as she can. She needs extra fluid while she breast-feeds.

44. How can Angela be sure she is producing enough milk?

If she has small breasts, she may be anxious that they are not adequate for the job. Small breasts can give as much milk as large breasts. The difference in size is due to fat. There are probably as many milk-producing glands in both sizes of breasts.

Breast-feeding is a matter of supply and demand. It is your *baby* who sets the quantity he wants and gets, not his mother. She should allow the demand to become established.

Many doctors suggest a starting time of 10 minutes or so at each breast. This is only a guideline. Your wife should not feel she has to stick rigidly to this. She should move your baby to the other breast when she feels he has emptied the supply from the first. If he has had enough, start him on the other breast at the next feeding.

Watch your baby. If his ears move a little while he is feeding, he is eating, not playing. Babies may feed more slowly from the breast than they do from the bottle. They may take short rest periods between sucking.

Try not to let doubts your wife has about an adequate milk supply deter her from breast-feeding. She can always obtain advice from her doctor.

45. Lilly is diabetic. Will she be able to breast-feed?

It's important for your wife to discuss this with her doctor. This is necessary due to hormonal changes following childbirth that may result in an altered insulin requirement.

The increased caloric intake required during breast-feeding may indicate a need for more insulin. Some mothers find their need for insulin decreases while breast-feeding. There is no evidence to show

breast milk of a diabetic mother is harmful to her
baby.

46. *Will Alice lose her figure if she breast-feeds?*

The shape of a woman's breasts changes with age.
Breast-feeding doesn't mean her bosom will get
droopy.

47. *Why does Anita get stomach cramps when she
breast-feeds our baby?*

This cramping feeling is caused by the muscles of
the uterus contracting as the womb returns to its
normal, prebirth size. The baby sucking at the breast
stimulates production of the hormone *oxytocin*. It
helps this contracting process. Within a couple of
weeks, these cramps will disappear.

48. *Daphne is complaining of cracked, sore nipples
because of breast-feeding. What can she do?*

This is not a sign she is failing to feed properly. The
nipple may not be far enough inside your baby's
mouth. The baby chews and drags on it, instead of
sucking.

A cold compress may help, and your wife could
wear a nipple shield. Rarely does severe *mastitis,*
inflammation of the breasts, occur due to an
infection. Consult the doctor if the discomfort
persists.

Your wife should not use soap on her nipples. She
should leave her breasts uncovered for a while each
day.

49. *Will any drugs or medicines Pat takes pass into the milk?*

Yes, certain drugs pass into breast milk. Your wife should be careful about any medications she takes. She should always consult her doctor first. Tranquilizers, nicotine, antibiotics, caffeine, aspirin and laxatives all affect the milk to some degree.

50. *Can alcohol pass to our baby through breast milk?*

A small amount of alcohol when breast-feeding shouldn't harm your baby. Your wife can enjoy a glass of wine or beer. It may even relax her before a feeding. But your wife shouldn't drink too much. Alcohol can pass through to the milk and make the baby woozy.

51. *Can some foods affect our baby if he is breast-fed?*

Some foods will affect your baby. Certain spicy foods can cause problems for the baby. Chocolate should be avoided, too.

Your wife should eat certain foods if she is breast-feeding. She will need fresh fruits and vegetables, and whole-wheat bread to help keep her digestive system working. She should also drink lots of fluid.

If your baby reacts to any food your wife is eating, you'll see signs of it. Your wife should not eat these foods while she is breast-feeding.

52. *Is it safe for Kay to smoke while she's breast-feeding?*

It is not advisable, because nicotine passes through to the milk. It may also reduce the milk supply.

53. *I've heard a woman's breasts may become engorged if she is breast-feeding. What does this mean?*

Sometimes, after her milk comes in, a woman's breasts become swollen, painful and overfull. The nipples seem to recede so it is difficult for the baby to feed. This is called *engorgement.*

If this happens, the best thing to do is have your wife express some milk, then let the baby feed. Showering may also help. It is sometimes easier to express milk if the breasts are warm.

She should not express more milk than necessary. Continued stimulation of the breasts may cause her to produce more milk. Breast massage may also help. After a feeding, a cold compress may be comforting.

54. *What is a let-down reflex?*

This term refers to the reflex that encourages the flow of milk from the breasts. When your baby begins to suck at the nipple, his mother's pituitary gland stimulates the release of oxytocin in her blood vessels. This causes the appropriate glands to squeeze out a supply of milk through the nipple. Your wife will be aware of the let-down reflex because it's accompanied by a sensation of warmth and a tingling feeling in the breasts.

55. *Is it true that a breast-feeding mother may sometimes leak milk?*

This may happen, due to the let-down reflex operating before the baby is put to the breast. The breasts may also become full. Sometimes it occurs in one breast while she is feeding with the other.

Most breast-feeding mothers experience leaking at some time. It can be dealt with by using special breast pads. If your wife puts the bottom of her hand over the nipple and pushes inward, she may find this stops the leaking.

56. *Is it easy to cope with breast-feeding when you are traveling?*

Breast-feeding when traveling is more convenient than bottle-feeding. You don't have bottles, nipples or formula to bring along. When traveling, warming a bottle or storing formula can be a problem. If you go by car, you can stop if your wife wants to feed or drive on as she does. Some airlines try to find an uncrowded area or private seat where a mother can feed comfortably and quietly.

57. *Betsy is worried about breast-feeding when she is out with the baby.*

Many women find this embarrassing, but in time it should be overcome. There is an art in breast-feeding without being obvious. This can soon be achieved. It's not really a mother's problem, but society's problem. Some stores and public buildings now have special areas in restrooms for nursing mothers. If your wife can't find one, she can use a quiet, warm corner somewhere. She can lift her sweater or undo her blouse modestly, and feed the baby.

58. *Our baby seems to favor one breast. Is this normal?*

This sometimes happens. Suggest to your wife that she offer the other breast first, encouraging him to suck for about 10 minutes. This will help build up the milk supply in that breast. She might also express some milk on that nipple to encourage him. Your wife can try holding the baby at a slightly different angle.

59. *Today our baby seemed to be struggling at the breast. Why does this happen?*

It may be the position he was in during feeding. Almost all the areola, the darker area of the breast, and the nipple should be in his mouth. Make sure he is comfortably cradled while at the breast.

Immediately after birth, he may be affected by pain-relieving drugs given during labor. If he is older, reluctance to take to the breast could be due to an infection.

If he was bottle-fed to start with, he may need some time to get used to his mother's natural milk. Talk with your doctor if the problem continues.

60. *I've heard a women can put her breast milk in a bottle. If she has to go out, someone else can feed the baby with her milk. Is that true?*

Yes, it's true. If your wife is breast-feeding and has to be away for a few hours, you may be able to feed the baby. All she has to do is express a quantity of milk by hand or with a breast pump. You can store it in a sterile container in a refrigerator up to 24 hours. Some breast pumps convert into a bottle. Your wife may need to express a certain amount of milk if her breasts become engorged. This means they are swollen, painful and overfull.

61. *Our baby was born by Caesarean section. Will Jane be able to breast-feed?*

There is no reason why your wife shouldn't breast-feed. If she had the Caesarean section under a general anesthetic, she may not be able to breast-feed immediately. She should ask for the baby as soon as she is fully awake. She may find it uncomfortable to hold the baby until the stitches heal.

62. Betty's breast milk is a blue-white color. Is this normal?

This is the normal color of healthy breast milk. You are probably more used to seeing the richer color of cow's milk. The first breast milk, colostrum, is creamier.

63. We are hoping to adopt a newborn baby. Will Mindy be able to breast-feed her?

Once a woman's breasts have given milk, they may be capable of producing it even years later. If your wife previously breast-fed a child of her own, she may be able to breast-feed this baby. The baby may need supplemental feedings with a bottle until you see whether your wife's milk is plentiful. This may take a few weeks. Breast-feeding may not be possible. Check with your doctor.

64. I have heard some women find breast-feeding a sexual experience. Is that true?

Breast-feeding does have a sensual aspect to it. Some women may even feel guilty about the physical pleasure it gives them. The breasts are a highly erogenous zone. Some women achieve orgasm from breast stimulation alone. There are reports of mothers who have reached a climax while breast-feeding. Most women experience a feeling of well-being after feeding.

65. How important is it for Sandy to wear a bra after the birth? She is breast-feeding.

During *lactation,* the period while she is breast-feeding, it's important for her to wear a good,

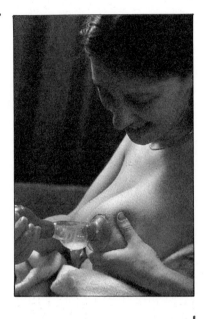

Breast milk is good for your baby. But you may feel left out because you can't feed him. Even if your wife is breast-feeding, you can feed the baby. You will be able to bottle-feed him when your wife expresses her breast milk.

well-fitting bra. A special nursing bra is useful. Heavier breasts need support. Wearing a bra at night may help her maintain her figure. A bra will also enable her to wear pads, in case leaking occurs.

Your wife may wear a nursing bra with flaps that can be undone. She should breast-feed topless when she can. Skin contact encourages milk flow.

66. *Cora doesn't know if she can breast-feed when she has a period.*

If in doubt, she should talk to her doctor. The menstrual cycle may not resume again while she is breast-feeding, but it may. There is probably no reason for your wife to stop breast-feeding. If your baby seems a little upset, it may be a reflection of his mother's premenstrual emotional state, not the milk.

67. *Our 3-year-old wants to suck at the breast again, too. What can we do about this?*

This is not an unfamiliar problem. Some children react to a newborn baby with overt jealousy. Others regress to babyhood in an attempt to attract your attention. It's probably best not to allow your child to compete with the baby this way.

Show your older child affection in other ways. Cuddle him when your wife cradles the baby as she breast-feeds. Explain to him only babies are fed this way. When he was a baby he was also fed that way. Now, he is bigger and eats like you.

TAKING CARE OF BABY

68. Does our baby need a bath every day?

Most parents like to bathe the baby every day, but it isn't necessary. When it's cold, twice a week is adequate, if you keep the baby clean between baths. You should wash his face a couple of times a day. There is no ideal time for bathing a baby.

69. I'd like to help at bath time. What can I do?

Make sure your hands are warm. Babies hate cold hands and usually respond by crying. Keep the room warm, because babies lose heat more quickly than adults. Bath water should be body temperature. You can test it with your elbow.

Before you start to bathe the baby, have everything you need at hand. *Never leave a baby alone in the bathtub or on a changing table.*

Undress your baby, and wrap him in a towel. Wash his face before you put him in the bath. Use cotton balls to wash his eyes. With cotton swabs, clean behind his ears and around his nose. Never push swabs in his ears or up a nostril. This could cause damage. Don't get soap in his eyes. Holding his head over the bath, wash his head with a sponge or cloth, using baby shampoo. Rinse and dry gently.

Give your baby a feeling of security by the confident way you hold him. Resting his head on your forearm, lower him into the water. Wash him with soap, then rinse it off. Play with him in the water, too.

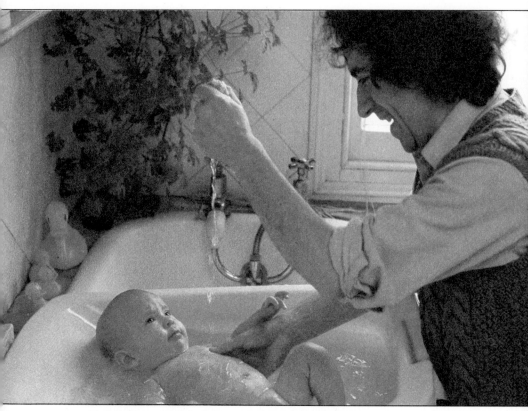

Bath time can be enjoyable for baby and parents. Most babies dislike a bath the first few weeks, but soon learn to enjoy it.

He may not like a bath at first, but he'll soon start to enjoy it. Wrap him in a towel and pat him dry. Keep him warm before you dress him. Powder and baby oil aren't necessary unless they are recommended for a rash or other condition.

70. *Can you give me some tips about changing our baby's diapers?*

During the first year of your baby's life, he will be changed over 4,000 times. Your wife will appreciate it if you can help her.

First, have everything ready. You will need baby wipes, baby oil or lotion, a diaper pail and a clean diaper. A changing mat is useful, but any flat surface will do.

Undo your baby's diaper. Wipe away any soiling, and clean his bottom with the baby wipes. Apply baby oil or lotion, if necessary. If you have a girl, wipe toward her bottom. There is less risk of infection entering the vagina or bladder. Put the diaper in solution to soak.

Disposable diapers are easy to put on. If you use cloth diapers, fold the diaper in a triangle or kite shape.

Preshaped diapers are easy to use, because they don't need folding. Diaper liners are useful, because they keep your baby from getting too wet. You can also use them inside disposable diapers. Not all disposable diapers can be flushed, so throw them in the garbage.

71. *Why do some people swaddle their babies?*

Swaddling is a form of wrapping. Studies show babies sleep better and are quieter when they are swaddled. It is as if being wrapped in a blanket gives babies a feeling of security. Accustomed to being curled up in the womb, a sudden sense of freedom may be unwelcome. A baby is also warmer if wrapped up. Babies lose heat quickly unless dressed and covered well. Their temperature is no longer that of the mother's body.

You may find wrapping a fussy baby in a blanket encourages him to sleep. But don't overdo things. Too many blankets may cause overheating.

72. *Our baby seems to vomit after a feeding. Why does he do this?*

Regurgitation of food in this way is common in small babies. It could be due to swallowed air. You may relieve this by burping him during a feeding. You could be overfeeding him. Overfeeding is not a risk in breast-fed babies.

There's a difference between spitting up and violent vomiting. Spitting up a bit is normal, as long as your baby is gaining weight well and otherwise thriving. Vomiting should be reported to your doctor. It could be a sign of something more serious.

73. *What should we do if our baby develops diarrhea?*

Diarrhea can be dangerous in a small baby, resulting in serious dehydration or loss of fluid. Signs of dehydration include:
- Dry mouth.
- Decreased or absent urination.
- Soft spot on head sunken in.
- No tears, if your baby usually has tears when crying.

Contact your doctor immediately if your baby shows signs of dehydration or if symptoms do not disappear or improve in 24 hours.

74. *Our baby seems constipated. What should we do?*

There is a difference between the stools of breast- and bottle-fed babies. A breast-fed baby has stools that are soft and yellow, with the consistency of applesauce. Stools of the bottle-fed baby are firmer.

Some babies will have six to eight stools a day, and some will go a couple of days without a stool. Either pattern is normal. If stools are extremely firm, consult your doctor. Never give a baby laxatives without seeking medical advice first!

75. *What is the correct position to use when we put our baby down to sleep?*

Put your baby down in one of three sleeping postures—on either side with his bottom tilted up or on his front with his head to one side. Alternate these positions. Never put him down on his back. If he spits up, he might choke.

Sleeping on his tummy is safest. If he spits up, it won't run down his throat and make him cough or choke. It'll run out of his mouth. If he wakes up and appears restless, put him in another position so he's more comfortable. If he's on his side, put a rolled diaper or blanket against his back to keep him from rolling over.

Within a few weeks, he may want to look around at his environment when he wakes up. He won't be able to see much on his front. If he seems frustrated in this position, turn him on his back when he's awake.

HANDLING BABY

76. *When I am dressing our baby, what should I keep in mind?*

Dressing a small baby is like dressing a floppy doll, except a doll keeps still. It gets easier with practice.

First, ease the clothes over his limbs. Don't push his arms and legs through the sleeves and legs of garments. It is also easier to gather up the sides of a garment that has to be put on over the head. Pass it over the back of his head. Slip it quickly over his face, so it isn't covered any longer than necessary.

The best garments to choose for your baby are loose and easy to put on and take off. They shouldn't be made of rough, irritating fabric. Avoid fluffy sweaters to avoid the possibility of inhaling some of the hair. Small fastenings and bulky seams are also unsuitable. A sleeper suit with covered feet helps keep the baby's legs and feet warm.

77. What is the correct way to burp our baby?

Whether your baby is breast- or bottle-fed, he will usually swallow some air. You can't prevent this. Some babies may be able to bring up their own burp, others need help. There are various ways to do this. Try one of the three methods described below:

1. Lay your baby across your knees, and gently rub or pat his back.

2. Sit him on your knee and rub or pat his back, while supporting him with your other hand.

3. Hold him upright against your shoulder and rub or pat his back.

If he hasn't burped within a couple of minutes, he probably doesn't need to. Discomfort may be due to crying, rather than causing it.

Colic is different from ordinary swallowed air. It occurs about the same time each day, often in the evening after feeding. A baby cries vehemently and becomes distressed. Doctors are not sure what causes colic. Seeing a baby screaming like this can be a frightening experience. Nothing will quiet him.

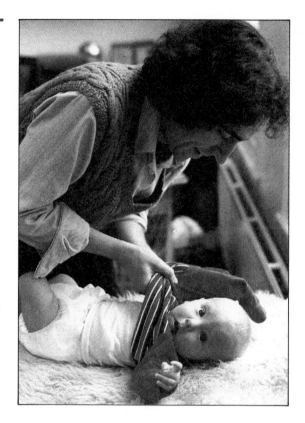

Dressing baby can be tricky until you learn how. Quickly put on or take off anything that has to be pulled over his head. Don't take too long dressing him. A newborn baby needs to be kept warm.

Some doctors believe colic may be caused by cow's milk in the breast-feeding mother's diet. If it becomes a problem, your wife can stop drinking milk for a few days to see if the colic attacks stop.

Call your doctor if you think your baby has colic. Encourage your wife to rest before the evening feeding. It may also help to feed the baby in a quiet, relaxed atmosphere.

78. What is the best way to carry our baby?

A baby can sense if the person carrying him is not fully confident. He may react by crying. You may have noticed this the first time you held your newborn. If he began to cry, you may have handed him to the nurse, only to find his crying stopped.

Your baby can't support his head, so you'll need to put one hand under it. Don't pick him up under his arms. Cradle him close to your body, with his head against your shoulder. In this position you can have eye contact. A cloth sling is a useful way to carry him when you're walking around. Some carriers can be worn at the front or on your back. Others have a metal frame. HPBooks' *Child Care From Birth To Age 5* has information about how to pick up and carry your baby and what equipment to buy.

79. Our new baby is small and fragile looking. I'm scared of picking her up because I feel so clumsy.

Your baby is dependent on you. It's not unusual to think of her as fragile, and you may be afraid you'll drop her. You may be anxious about the navel as it heals. She can't coordinate her movements to help you change or bathe her.

With normal, careful handling you won't harm her. You probably know instinctively how to hold her. Regular, close contact helps cement the parent-child relationship.

YOUR BABY'S NEEDS

80. Does our newborn really need all that sleep?

Your baby is developing at a considerable rate, both physically and mentally. Sleep is vital for growth. You will find he sleeps from feeding to

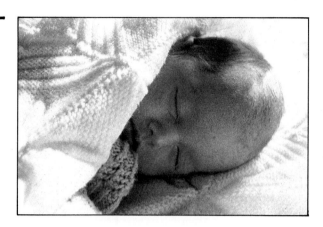

For the first few weeks, your baby may sleep from feeding to feeding. As he develops, the time he remains awake increases. The safest way for him to lie is on his stomach or side.

feeding for the first few weeks. He may even fall asleep while he's eating. This is normal. Enjoy it while you can. Before long, you may be exhausted by all the energy he has.

81. *What type of crib would you recommend for our baby?*

Under U.S. and Canadian regulations, a crib must meet certain standards. Check out any bed you buy to see if it meets established standards. HPBooks' *Child Care From Birth To Age 5* contains information about cribs and other equipment for babies.

82. *How important it is for the house to be quiet while our baby is sleeping?*

Your newborn baby will spend a lot of time sleeping for the next few months. If you keep silence as the rule, life will be difficult. Carry on as normal. Let him get used to the background sound of the radio, television, telephone and other household equipment. He'll sleep soundly through it all.

83. *Should the baby sleep in our room?*

It depends on how you feel about it. It's all right for a baby to sleep in his own room. He can also sleep in a bassinet in your room for the first couple of months. After that, he may disturb you. When he is in his own room, leave the door open so you can hear him.

84. *Donna thinks it would be better for the baby to sleep in our bed. Do you think this is a good idea?*

No, this is not a good idea. Parents could roll over in their sleep and accidentally smother the baby. What about a compromise? Have your baby in the room with you, in a bassinet.

85. *Does our baby need a pillow?*

Pillows are unnecessary. They may cause suffocation and are not recommended for the first year. When you do start using one, put it *under* the sheet.

86. *Should we leave the window open in the baby's room when he's sleeping?*

In warm weather, it's fine to do this. When it's cold, it could be dangerous. The temperature can drop suddenly at night. Cold weather can bring the danger of hypothermia for a baby and risk of sudden death. Overheating should also be avoided. Check the temperature in your baby's room. It should be about 75F (25C) when you first bring him home. After a time, you could keep it at 68F to 70F (20C to 21C).

87. *How often should we weigh our baby?*

If you have a baby scale at home, don't weigh him

every day. You might become obsessive about his progress. Weighing him once a week or every two weeks should be adequate. He will be weighed when he sees the doctor for his regular checkups.

88. I've heard pacifiers are not good for babies. Is that true?

Some people don't like the look of a pacifier in a baby's mouth. Some say pacifiers are unhygenic. Others feel pacifying a baby is better than letting him cry. The sound of his own crying may disturb him even more. Still others think a baby should suck his thumb, not a pacifier. But there is no evidence a pacifier does any harm.

The sucking instinct is usually strong in a newborn. It is the means by which he gets his food. A baby may need to satisfy this instinct even when he is not hungry. That could be what persistent crying is about, when it occurs after a feeding and is not due to swallowed air.

Even if you give your baby a pacifier, you may find he rejects it. Some babies do.

BABY'S HEALTH

89. What will our newborn's first physical examinations show?

During the 24 hours following birth, your baby will be weighed and measured. His head will be examined and reflexes will be tested. His ears, eyes, nose and mouth will be looked at. His heart, lungs and abdomen will be checked.

The doctor will feel the soft spots on his head, called the *fontanelles.* He will check for sign of congenital dislocation of the hip. In a baby girl, the

All babies have a strong sucking instinct. Whether you let your infant suck his thumb or give him a pacifier is a matter of choice.

vaginal area will be examined. In a boy, the scrotum will be looked at to see if testicles have descended.

Any molding of the head is probably due to pressure from the uterus and vaginal walls during birth. The shape of the head will become more normal looking. Babies delivered by Caesarean section and breech babies usually have rounder heads.

At checkups during the first two months, your baby will be re-examined and an assessment will be made of his growth and development. He will also begin his course of immunizations at 2 months old.

90. *Claire told me after our baby was born the hospital did a blood test on him. What was it for?*

This test is carried out after delivery to check for a condition known as *phenylketonuria (PKU)* and also for underactivity of the thyroid gland. Both may result in abnormal development if not treated immediately. The test involves taking a small sample of blood from the baby's heel. Some states or provinces also screen for additional metabolic diseases.

91. *One of the tests the pediatrician did after the birth was for sign of congenital dislocation of the hip. Is this important?*

Babies are tested for this at birth and later exams. If the condition is found early enough, it can easily be treated.

Instead of the thigh bone fitting into the hip joint, it slips out. Treatment involves pinning diapers a certain way or putting legs into casts. Baby can be home rather than in the hospital while this treatment is being done.

92. *Why do some babies develop jaundice?*

Jaundice is common in the newborn. It's estimated to occur in about 50% of all babies. It usually shows itself in the first two to three days of life, then disappears in a week or so. Premature babies are most prone to it, and the condition may last longer. Your doctor will tell you if your baby has jaundice.

The most common type of jaundice is *physiologic jaundice.* When the newborn's surplus red-blood cells are broken down, a substance known as *bilirubin* is made. Sometimes the liver enzymes are not mature enough to cope with metabolizing the bilirubin. This yellow pigment of the bilirubin gives the baby's skin and eyes a yellow color. Once the baby's liver function improves, jaundice disappears. Other causes of jaundice in the newborn include blood-group incompatibility, other blood diseases, infection and certain liver and metabolic diseases.

Fortunately, most jaundice is mild and does not require specific therapy. However, in severe cases, the bilirubin level is high and there is danger of brain damage. To prevent the bilirubin level from becoming dangerously high, the doctor may use *phototherapy.* This is a form of light treatment. The wavelength in the light helps break down the bilirubin. If phototherapy is used, the baby is blindfolded so his eyes are not exposed to the light. Occasionally, the bilirubin level may continue to rise, in spite of phototherapy. Then a special type of blood transfusion is necessary.

93. *Our baby's eyes seem inflamed. Is this anything to worry about?*

Sometimes when the eyes receive medication immediately after birth, it causes the inflammation. The inflammation may also be due to infection. One of the principal signs of this is the eyelids tend to stick together, particularly after sleep, and there is a discharge that looks like pus. Consult your doctor.

94. *How should we treat diaper rash?*

When diaper rash occurs, it's usually due to some irritant, usually the diaper. It may be due to the washing detergent or soaking solution.

There may be substances in the stool that cause irritation. Your baby's diapers may not be changed often enough. Occasionally the baby will acquire a skin infection in the diaper area. Try to find the cause.

Exposing your baby's bottom to fresh air will help if he has diaper rash. Wash the area gently, and dry it by dabbing, not rubbing. Soothe the area with a cream recommended by your doctor. Change baby's diapers regularly. The baby is probably uncomfortable, so handle him tenderly.

95. *When will our baby need to be immunized?*

Immunization involves injecting the baby with a weak or inactivated substance of the disease from which he will be protected. The injection is usually given in the thigh. Antibodies are formed so when the baby is exposed to the disease, his system can resist it.

The principal diseases a baby is immunized against in the first year are diphtheria, whooping cough, tetanus and polio. A dose of each is required at 2, 4, 6 and 18 months. Immunization against measles, mumps and rubella is given at 15 months. Your baby may also be given a tuberculosis skin test at 1 year.

Immunization is the best way to protect your child's health. If there is anything in your medical history to suggest there may be a risk involved, consult your doctor.

Your doctor will give you a form for keeping a written record of the vaccinations your baby has and the date of each. Proof of immunizations are necessary before your child can start school.

96. *Is there any way we can tell our baby's temperature without using a thermometer?*

It's difficult to get an accurate reading without taking a rectal temperature. Taking the temperature in the armpit or groin is not always accurate. If your baby is ill, your doctor will probably ask what his *rectal* temperature is.

When you take your child in for regular checkups, ask the nurse how to take a rectal temperature. She'll be glad to show you how to do it.

97. *When is it necessary to call the doctor if we think the baby is ill?*

With experience, you'll learn this. Until then, call your doctor if your baby has a rectal temperature of 101F (38.4C) or higher, skips more than one feeding, feeds poorly or seems ill in some other way. It's always better to ask your doctor's opinion.

98. *What medicines are safe to give our baby?*

Don't give your baby *any* medications without discussing it with your doctor first.

99. *Does our newborn baby need vitamin supplements?*

Certain vitamin supplements are added to formula. If your baby is bottle-fed, he will get these. Most doctors recommend supplementary vitamins for breast-fed babies. These are taken as drops.

100. *Does our baby need extra iron?*

If your baby is bottle-fed, he should be on formula with iron. Some physicians prescribe vitamins with iron for breast-fed babies. Premature babies will also be given additional vitamin and iron supplements.

101. *Should we be concerned about our baby's weight?*

It used to be the larger the baby, the prouder the parents. But we now know fat babies are not only flabby and less active, but probably less healthy. There is strong evidence that a fat baby grows to be a fat child and a fat adult.

Weight gain is related to food intake. Your doctor may advise you to be careful about this if your baby is large. A breast-fed baby is rarely overweight.

YOUR MARRIAGE RELATIONSHIP

102. *How soon after the birth will we be able to resume sexual relations?*

There is no specific amount of time. If an episiotomy was performed, allow your wife to decide when she is comfortable. Penetration may cause some discomfort the first few times. Gentleness and lubrication will help, and normal sexual relations will be resumed easily. If there are problems, bring them to your doctor's attention.

103. *Is it true Jane can't conceive again while breast-feeding?*

A breast-feeding mother may find regular periods do not resume again until she weans the baby. Breast-feeding cuts down risk of conception, but it is *not* a safe method of contraception. Ovulation can occur two weeks *before* the first menstrual period after the birth. The rhythm method of contraception is also unreliable. It may be some time before regular menstruation resumes.

104. *Elsie decided she would prefer to be fitted with a diaphragm. How soon after the birth can this be done?*

The question of contraception requires consultation with your doctor. If your wife has used a diaphragm before, she may need a larger size now. A diaphragm can't usually be fitted until about six weeks after birth. Your wife can ask about this at her first postnatal checkup.

You may wish to use another form of contraception or refrain from intercourse. A diaphragm is only successful as a means of birth control if used carefully with spermicidal creams.

You may find an IUD, an intra-uterine device, is recommended. It is usually easier to fit after a woman has had a child.

105. *How soon after the birth can Fran start taking the pill?*

This is a matter for discussion with your doctor. Most women can take birth-control pills almost immediately after delivery. Some women may not for a variety of reasons. Breast-feeding is not a contraindication to taking the pill. Heavy smokers and women over 40 probably should not take the pill. If they do take the pill, they should be aware they may have more problems than other women.

106. *Do you recommend an intra-uterine device (IUD) as a method of contraception following the birth of our first child? We do not want more children for two or three years.*

There are various types of IUDs that can be fitted. Originally, they were made of metal, but now plastic is used more often. Most have a string that hangs down so the woman or her doctor can feel if it's in place. It shouldn't be felt by you during intercourse.

No one knows exactly how an IUD works. It's an effective method of contraception, although not 100% safe. Pregnancy can occur while the device is in position.

Some women experience prolonged bleeding and

pain with an IUD. They should have it removed and use another method of contraception. It won't usually be inserted until several weeks after the birth. Another form of contraception will have to be used until then.

Your wife should talk to her doctor about using an IUD. He will advise her of any problems and discuss different types.

107. *We've just had our first child. How safe is the withdrawal method of contraception?*

This method of contraception is known as *coitus interruptus*. The penis is withdrawn prior to ejaculation. The success of this method depends on the cooperation of both partners. The male's ability to sense impending ejaculation is important. He must remove the penis from the vagina prior to ejaculation. The woman may also be able to sense his feelings at this time and can help in the disengaging process.

But there are drawbacks to using this method. Your wife may not ovulate after the birth for a while. You can't be sure when she is fertile again. She could conceive during the two weeks before her first menstrual period following the birth.

There is a risk that ejaculation may occur prematurely in the vagina. Even if you do withdraw, the fluid secreted before actual ejaculation may contain some sperm.

If ejaculation occurs outside the vagina, it's still possible for sperm to travel up to the uterus. You may also find withdrawal is not favored by either of you.

Intercourse may be unsatisfactory because of the strain imposed. Your wife may find she can't reach orgasm. This method of contraception is unreliable any time.

108. *We have decided not to extend our family after the birth of our third baby. I am thinking of having a vasectomy. Would you advise this?*

There are many advantages to this form of contraception. The operation is a simple one. In some instances, it is reversible. In most cases, it is *not* reversible, so regard it as irreversible.

A vasectomy involves cutting and tying the *vas deferens*, the tube along which the sperm travel to the penis. It's usually performed under a local anesthetic on an out-patient basis. If it's done under general anesthesia, you wouldn't spend longer than a day in the hospital.

You'll need to use some other form of contraception afterward. Sperm may remain stored in the body for several weeks. Tests are done by the doctor to check this.

109. *Carolyn is worried because she doesn't feel maternal toward our baby.*

It isn't always love-at-first-sight. Even if she feels confident during pregnancy, your wife has to get used to the *reality* of being a mother. It isn't easy for everyone.

She may have no experience handling a baby and is fearful she can't cope. She needs time to develop the new relationship. Talking openly about anxieties will help her.

You need time to get to know your baby. Make it a shared experience. Today, fathers play an important part in the care of a baby during the first few months of life. Your wife needs your help and you'll enjoy the experience.

Not every parent immediately feels the "parental" instinct. Bonding is sometimes more gradual. It is reinforced as you spend more time with your infant, having close physical contact with him.

110. *I'm feeling left out of things, even jealous. Sandy is giving so much attention to the baby. Do most new fathers feel this way at times?*

The birth of your baby has been an emotional time for you. Everyone is making a fuss over your wife and the baby. This may add to your feelings of resentment.

You'll feel better if you become involved with the care of your baby. Even the most capable woman needs and appreciates her husband's help with a new baby. Talk to your wife about feelings of jealousy. Bottled-up resentment isn't healthy.

111. *Will Karen suffer postnatal depression? If so, how can I help her through it?*

The *baby blues,* as it is called, often occurs a few days after birth. The weepy feeling disappears quickly. Most new mothers experience the blues, so your wife shouldn't be embarrassed if she wants to cry.

There are many reasons why the reaction may occur. It may be due to hormonal changes or the result of exertion during birth. A mother may feel anxious about her ability to cope. She may have feeding problems.

True postnatal depression is different. There may be signs of intense irritability and insomnia, as well as violent swings of mood. Everything may be perceived in an exaggerated way. The simplest thing takes on great significance. If this type of depression occurs, seek your doctor's advice.

In the meantime, make a fuss over her. Find someone to look after the baby for a few hours, and let your wife relax in bed. The worst thing you can do is tell her to "snap out of the depression." It isn't possible. Treat yourselves to an evening out together, because depression may be infectious.

There is evidence severe postnatal depression is less likely to occur if a woman has support from her husband, relatives and friends.

Don't be too surprised if you find *yourself* suffering from the blues while your wife is still in hospital. You'll probably want her to come home and hate feeling like a hospital visitor.

112. *Ruth is feeling low. The baby is disturbing her nights so much that she hardly sleeps at all. Is there anything we can do?*

You both have to be prepared to lose some sleep for

the first few months. It's part of being a new parent. Your baby isn't being difficult because he wakes up at night. Some babies sleep through the night early, others need a night feeding for a few months.

Share the burden with your wife as much as possible. There isn't a lot you can do if the baby is breast-fed during the night. If the baby is bottle-fed, you can feed him every other night.

You may find delaying the last feeding will help. If you bottle-feed, make the bottle in advance. Then you'll only lose a few minutes sleep in the middle of the night. If your baby wakes every two or three hours, you have more of a problem. Talk to your doctor about it.

Try to get your wife to take a nap during the day. Encourage her to take as much help as is offered from relatives and friends. She needs as much rest as possible after the birth. Doing relaxation exercises she learned at prenatal classes may also help. She should be eating sensibly during this time. You should both go to bed as early as you can.

113. *Since the birth of our baby two months ago, Georgia has become cold toward me in our lovemaking. What could be causing this?*

Try to be understanding. It may take a while for a woman's sexual interest to return following childbirth. She needs time to readjust. There have been many changes in her body over the last few months.

She may also be feeling uncomfortable because of her stitches. She should talk to her doctor if they are too tight. If any pain is felt internally during intercourse, encourage her to talk to her doctor about it. You may need to use a lubricant if her normal vaginal secretions are not yet present. A different position for intercourse may be more comfortable.

Communication about each other's feelings often solves problems that arise between people. Try to talk about your problems and feelings. You will have to take time to work things out.

Your wife might be afraid of getting pregnant again. If this is the case, she should talk to her doctor about contraceptive use.

Making love after childbirth is a new experience for *both* of you. With patience, you may find a new tenderness. Lovemaking may be more satisfying for both of you than ever before.

114. *What will our daily routine be like when the baby comes home?*

Your first few weeks at home with the baby will be exciting, but exhausting. The reality of being a parent 24 hours a day may strike you suddenly. Most couples quickly establish a routine. Try to remain flexible, because your routine will change as your baby develops. Below is a sample routine. Use it as a model, and alter it to suit both your needs:

6 a.m.

Early feeding. Change his diaper, then back to bed for an extra hour's sleep.

7:30 a.m.

Get up and eat a good breakfast together. Help with some housework if you can.

9 a.m.

Change and bathe the baby. Prepare a bottle if bottle-feeding.

10 a.m.

Morning feeding and diaper change. If your baby is sleepy, put him down for a rest. If not, spend time cuddling and playing with him.

10:45 a.m.

Your wife should have a break. It's important for her to be well-rested after the birth. Caring for a new baby can be tiring.

11:30 a.m.

Housework, but don't let your wife become obsessive about it. Tell her you don't want her to overdo things. Clean equipment if bottle-feeding. Prepare lunch.

1 p.m.

Remind your wife to stop for lunch, then rest.

2 p.m.

Early afternoon feeding and change the baby. Cuddle and play with him.

3 p.m.

Take the baby for a walk or go shopping.

4:30 p.m.

Begin to prepare dinner.

6 p.m.

Evening bath and feeding. Diaper change.

7:30 p.m.

Evening meal.

10 p.m.

Last feeding of the day and diaper change. Play with the baby if you weren't home for the 6 p.m. feeding.

11 p.m.

Bedtime. You may have to be up again at 2 a.m. for a feeding, so try to sleep before then.

OTHER QUESTIONS ABOUT BABY

115. *When I was born, my mother says she was in bed for two weeks. This isn't the practice today, is it?*

The period following the birth is called the *puerperium* and lasts from six to eight weeks. In the past, it was thought a woman was unclean during this time, because of the *lochia* discharge that comes after childbirth. She was kept isolated and confined to bed.

Today, doctors want to get the new mother up as quickly as possible after birth. This will help her feel better faster. She still needs rest, but the exercise provided by walking around is beneficial.

116. *What is a caul?*

Rarely, a baby is born without the membranes having ruptured. They cover his face, and the covering is known as the *caul.*

117. *We can't agree about a name for our child. Are there any points to bear in mind?*

This is a big responsibility. Your child will have to live with the name you choose. Many people feel the names they give their children set their characters to some extent.

Consider whether a popular name will date quickly. Avoid embarrassing initials, too. Paul Nutt sounds fine, but P. Nutt will haunt him all his life!

You may wish to name your child after someone you are fond of or use your wife's surname as a middle name. You might also combine part of your wife's name with part of yours, to form something more original.

If you are having problems choosing a name, HPBooks' *Big Book of Baby Names* has more than 13,000 names and variations to choose from. It might make selection easier!

118. *Can we spoil our baby at this early stage?*

It's not possible to spoil a baby who is only a few weeks old. If he cries, it's for a reason. He is hungry, uncomfortable or needs attention. Later he may start to make demands for your attention by yelling. There may be a risk, especially with a first baby, of spoiling him if you submit to his whims too readily.

119. *What things should we keep in mind when traveling with our baby?*

Disposable is the key word when traveling. Take disposable diapers, tissues and baby wipes. Disposable bottles and disposable nipples are also useful if your wife is bottle-feeding. You can even take premixed formula in cans!

If you are traveling by public transportation, get the best seat. Service will be better. It will be less crowded and you will be more comfortable.

If you're going by car, put your baby in a car restraint. It will protect him in case of an accident. HPBook's *Child Care From Birth To Age 5* covers car restraints and safety seats in detail.

120. *Will our baby be right- or left-handed?*

This isn't anything to be bothered about so early. In the first year or so, you may notice he uses both hands and is ambidextrous. Later, he will begin to use one hand more than the other. If he shows preference for his left hand as a baby, he may be left-handed. Trying to persuade an obviously left-handed child to use his right hand is not encouraged. It may only confuse him.

Some people think being left-handed is a handicap. Some of the world's greatest artists, actors, businessmen, musicians and sportsmen have been *sinistrals*. That's another term for someone who is left-handed.

121. *Do you think it's possible for parents to love all their children equally?*

It's probably a matter of how you define the word "love." All children have individual personalities and enjoy different relationships with their parents. You may find yourself feeling differently about each of them. You appreciate their unique qualities, sometimes because of their faults. The extent of your devotion will be similar.

122. *Is a second child easier to manage?*

A second child is probably not more content than a first. What is different is the parents' ability to understand a baby's needs and reactions. This is a result of experience. Confidence increases after coping with the first child.

123. *What sort of stroller would you recommend?*

There are many types on the market. The one you buy depends on how much money you want to spend. It's convenient to have a stroller that folds and has a carrying handle.

Another good way to carry your baby is in a

carrying sling. This can be a convenient way of getting around. Some slings have a frame and are worn on the back. Some are designed for front carrying, others can be worn either way. Be sure there is nothing sharp on the carrier. The frame and fabric must also be strong.

124. *Is it true fluoride will make our baby's teeth stronger?*

There is evidence that prescribing a tiny dose for the mother during pregnancy may help prevent tooth decay in the baby later. In some places, fluoride is added to the water supply. If there is no fluoride in your local water supply, fluoride supplements will be prescribed for your baby.

125. *Is it ever safe to leave our baby alone?*

It isn't necessary for you to have him in sight *all* the time. It's safe to leave him in his room, on the patio or in the yard if he is protected. But someone should always be within hearing range, in case he starts to cry.

Never leave him alone at home, even if you think you're going to be gone only a few minutes. Something could happen to you. Never leave him in his stroller outside a store or supermarket, either.

126. *Do babies dream?*

Research shows we all dream every night. Whether or not we remember our dream depends on when we wake up. Our periods of dreaming may be essential to psychological stability. Dreams are accompanied by rapid eye movement, also called *REM.*

Watch your baby while he is sleeping. You will notice his eyeballs move underneath the lids. This is a sign of REM sleep. Your baby may not be dreaming the same way we do. But periods of rapid eye movement may be as important to an infant as they are to an adult.

127. *I've heard of something called witch's milk. What is it?*

Sometimes parents notice a baby has enlarged breasts, which secrete a little fluid. This is known as *witch's milk*. It is caused by hormones that have passed from the mother, through the placenta, to the baby. No treatment is necessary. It's nothing to be concerned about and soon disappears.

128. *We have a pool and I'm afraid the baby may fall in it when he's older. We've heard we can teach our baby to swim at a very early age. Is this true?*

There are classes available to help you teach your child to be watersafe. Some of these are held at your local YWCA and YMCA and are for children as young as 3 months old. If you have trouble finding a class in your area, HPBooks' *How to Watersafe Infants and Toddlers* is an excellent book to use to make your baby watersafe.

129. *Ilsa is expecting again and is still feeding our first child. Can she continue to do this?*

There is no reason why she shouldn't breast-feed through the pregnancy. In some countries, mothers breast-feed both the older child and a new baby.

Your wife may find her milk supply decreases during the pregnancy due to hormonal changes. She should be guided by her own observation and feelings. Your wife should also discuss this with her doctor.

Jealousy of the new baby may be overcome if you include the older child in the care of the new baby. Let the child take pride in being older. Set aside time alone with the older child.

130. *Our 3-year-old seems jealous of the new baby. How can we help her cope now that she is no longer an only child?*

A new baby can lead to many emotional responses. At first, you may have found your 3-year-old wanted to hold and touch the baby. She was affectionate toward him. Then things may have changed, as she became aware of how much of your time he was taking. Resentment may show itself in bedwetting, tantrums or displays of anger toward the baby. If things reach this extreme, don't leave the two of them alone together.

Much of this will depend on your relationship as parents with your older child before the birth. It may be influenced by the way you prepare her for his arrival. Your wife will need to spend a lot of her time with the baby. It may fall to you to give your daughter the extra love and special attention she needs.

Try to involve your older child in caring for the baby. She can help change diapers and do other tasks. You will have to adjust to being a family of four.

131. *Harriet has been home for three days and has suddenly developed a high temperature. Should we call the doctor?*

Your doctor will want to see her. The fever may be a sign of an infection. Call him immediately.

132. *How easy will it be for Linda to get her figure back after the birth?*

She will feel lighter immediately after the birth. Like most new mothers, she may be conscious of a thickened waist, heavier thighs and a larger bosom, especially if she is breast-feeding. Her face, wrists and ankles may also be plumper.

Strict dieting following the birth should be avoided. A well-balanced diet is essential for your wife to maintain her health and the baby's if she is breast-feeding.

If she is not breast-feeding, a low-carbohydrate diet may be necessary. She will need to exercise regularly during the weeks following the birth to regain her figure. Postnatal exercises may tone abdomen muscles.

Encourage your wife to set aside a time each day to exercise. Walking 20 minutes a day is another form of exercise for the period immediately after the birth.

133. *Can you recommend some exercises I could practice with Joy to help her regain her figure? I'd like to tighten up my stomach muscles, too.*

Your wife will probably have to work on overstretched stomach muscles and posture following the birth. It's a good idea for you both to follow a daily exercise program. Your wife may be given instructions in postnatal exercises in the hospital.

Encourage your wife to do post-natal exercises. She should regain her figure within a couple of months if she eats a well-balanced diet. Join in the exercises with her. You may lose a few pounds.

Exercise 1—For a flatter abdomen, lie on the bed with your knees drawn up. Breathe deeply and slowly. Draw in your stomach muscles. Hold, relax and breathe out. Turn on your right side and repeat. Repeat on your left side.

Exercise 2—Lie on the bed with your knees drawn up. Keep your feet flat on the bed. Lift your head and shoulders, and touch your knees. Relax.

Exercise 3—Lie on the bed with your knees drawn up. Raise one leg and then the other. Relax.

Exercise 4—Lie on the bed with your knees drawn up. Roll the knees to the left. Twist your right hip off the bed, keeping shoulders down. Repeat, holding the knees to the right.

Other Exercises—Simple bending and stretching exercises are also useful. Repeat them several times, morning and evening. If you are exercising properly, you should feel muscles contracting.

If your wife had a Caesarean section or there is some doubt about her fitness, consult your doctor.

134. *My mother-in-law has taken over our household since Kate came home with the baby. She only came to stay for three weeks, but it's too much. Kate is also beginning to resent the excessive attention.*

Your mother-in-law probably thinks your household couldn't run without her now. The three weeks will soon be over. Your wife could try explaining you need to be alone together. Send your mother-in-law on errands so you can have some time together.

Grandparents play a valuable role in family life. Many have a lot to offer in terms of advice and help. But you need to set a framework for the role from the beginning. Then they won't become overwhelming with their attentions and affections.

135. *What should a parent know about first-aid and emergency care of an infant?*

Although an emergency may never occur, there are some things you should know how to do. Cardiopulmonary resuscitation (CPR) is very important for a parent to know. It involves breathing for the child and keeping the blood circulating in the body if these functions have ceased. Choking is another area you need to know how to deal with, especially as your child grows older. Soon he will be putting everything in his mouth. HPBooks' *How to Save a Life Using CPR* is a good book to use to learn these techniques.

Grandparents may have a lot of advice to offer. Be sure they don't take over your new family completely. The first few weeks at home with your baby are tiring. Make the most of offers of help, so you and your wife can have some time together.

Other accidents and emergencies include bleeding, cuts, burns, broken bones, sprained ankles. HPBooks' *Child Care From Birth To Age 5* contains a complete, well-illustrated accidents-and-emergency section that covers various situations. The book also contains an illustrated illness section covering 113 different childhood diseases and illnesses.

Glossary of Terms

Abortion—Spontaneous or induced delivery of the embryo or fetus.

Amniocentesis—A test taking a sample of amniotic fluid surrounding the fetus in the womb. Fluid is removed through the abdominal wall of the mother. This sample is examined for birth defects, determination of sex and other tests.

Amniotomy—Artificial rupture of the amniotic sac.

Anemia—Deficiency in red-blood cells or hemoglobin, which carry oxygen through the body.

Anesthesia—*General* anesthesia causes loss of consciousness and sensation. *Local* anesthesia produces loss of sensation in a particular area. It does not involve loss of consciousness.

Antibodies—Substances produced by the body for protection from certain diseases or infections.

Braxton-Hicks Contractions—Painless contractions that occur during pregnancy. Do not confuse these with labor contractions.

Caesarean Section—Delivery of a baby by surgical means through the mother's abdomen. Also called *C-section*.

Caul—Piece of amniotic membrane that still covers the baby. It is a rare occurrence.

Cervix—Neck or lower part of the uterus.

Chromosomes—Rod-shape structures that are found in the nucleus of all the body's cells in 23 pairs. They contain genes, which are responsible for the development of hereditary characteristics.

Circumcision—Removal of the foreskin from the penis.

Colostrum—First milk produced by the breasts. It's rich in protein and antibodies, and provides a degree of immunity for the baby.

Contractions—Tightening of the uterus muscles during pregnancy and, more painfully, labor.

Crowning—Appearance of the baby's head in the vagina just prior to birth.

Diabetes—Condition where the pancreas fails to produce insulin, which is needed for converting carbohydrates, sugars and starches to energy.

Eclampsia—Serious form of pre-eclampsia that may occur if the condition is left untreated. Symptoms are vomiting, severe headache and seizure.

Edema—Swelling of various part of the body, especially hands and feet. Due to fluid retention.

Embryo—Term for newly conceived baby until the seventh week of gestation.

Enema—Way to empty the bowel by injecting fluid into it.

Epidural—Form of local anesthesia. Anesthesia is injected into the epidural space in the lower spinal region without loss of consciousness.

Episiotomy—Incision in the perineum to facilitate delivery of the baby's head.

Estrogen—Female sex hormone produced by the ovaries.

Fallopian Tubes—Two tubes that link the ovaries to the uterus.

Fetus—Name of the developing baby from the seventh week after conception until birth.

Fontanelles—Soft areas in the baby's skull.

Guthrie Test—Blood test done on all babies after birth to check for phenylketonuria (PKU), a rare condition causing mental handicap.

Gynecologist—Doctor who specializes in women's health.

Hemoglobin—Protein responsible for the color of red-blood cells. It carries oxygen around the body.

Hemorrhage—Loss of blood.

Hormones—Chemical messengers of the body.

Hypertension—High blood pressure.

Hypotension—Low blood pressure.

Intravenous Drip—Also called *I.V.* Means of introducing substances directly into the bloodstream through a fine tube inserted in a vein.

Jaundice—Condition in which the liver is immature or fails to work efficiently. A substance called *bilirubin* accumulates, causing a yellow tinge to the skin.

Lactation—Producing milk for breast-feeding.

Lanugo—Hair on the body of the fetus. Some hair may remain after birth, but is soon lost.

Lochia—Discharge from the vagina after childbirth. At first it's bright red, then gradually becomes paler.

Meconium—First excretion from the bowel of the newborn child.

Menstruation—Flow of blood from the womb about every 28 days. Absence of menstruation is often the first sign of pregnancy.

Miscarriage—Spontaneous delivery of the embryo or fetus before it can survive on its own.

Molding—Temporary alteration in the shape of the baby's head as it passes through the birth canal.

Multigravida—Mother who has already had one child.

Nausea—Unpleasant feeling of sickness.

Obstetrician—Doctor who specializes in the care of women during pregnancy and delivery of babies.

Orgasm—Sexual climax.

Ovulation—Monthly release of an egg from the ovary.

Ovum—Egg cell.

Oxytocin—Hormone used to stimulate contractions of the uterus.

Pediatrician—Doctor who specializes in the care of babies and children.

Perineum—Area between vulva and woman's anus.

Pica—Cravings in pregnancy to eat substances that are not food, such as coal or earth.

Pitocin—Brand name of *oxytocin,* which stimulates uterine contractions.

Placenta—Also known as the *afterbirth.* The structure that connects the fetus to the uterus, through which the fetus obtains nourishment and oxygen.

Placenta Previa—This condition occurs when the placenta lies over the cervix, partially or fully blocking the birth canal.

Postnatal—Period after the birth.

Pre-Eclampsia—Condition that may arise in pregnancy. Symptoms include high blood pressure, severe edema and protein in the urine.

Premature Baby—Baby weighing under 5-1/2 pounds or born before the 38th week of pregnancy.

Prenatal—Nine months of pregnancy before birth.

Presentation—Part of the baby's body that is born first. A head presentation is most common.

Primigravida—Medical term used to refer to a mother over age 30, expecting her first child.

Progesterone—Hormone produced by the ovaries.

Puerperium—Four-to-six-week period following childbirth.

Rhesus (Rh) Factor—Also called *Rh-factor.* A factor found in red-blood corpuscles. We have either Rh-positive or Rh-negative blood.

Roughage—Aids digestion and helps prevent constipation. Found in unrefined cereals, whole-wheat bread, raw vegetables and fruit. It is an important part of a healthy diet.

Sperm—Male seeds ejaculated at orgasm. A sperm must fertilize the egg for conception to occur.

Toxemia—Another term for pre-eclampsia. The full term is *pre-eclampsic toxemia.*

Ultrasound Scan—Picture of the fetus obtained by means of high-frequency sound waves.

Umbilical Cord—Cord that connects the baby to the placenta.

Urethra—Opening permitting the passing of urine from the bladder.

Uterus—Womb enlarges in pregnancy and contains the developing fetus.

Vagina—Passage leading from the outside to the cervix and the uterus. The penis enters the vagina during sexual intercourse.

Vasectomy—Method of male sterilization.

Vernix—White substance protecting the baby's skin in the womb. It is often still apparent at birth.

Vitamins—Chemical substances found in food. Essential for healthy growth and development.

Vulva—External female genitalia.

INDEX